Catholic Order of the Holy Mass

An Easy-to-Follow Guide to Understand and Fully Participate in the Prayers and Responses of the Catholic Mass

Benjamin Blakewell

GRAPEVINE BOOKS

Published by

GRAPEVINE BOOKS

www.grapevinebooks.com

email: contact@grapevinebooks.com

Ordering Information:

Quantity sales: Special discounts are available on quantity purchases

by corporations, associations, and others.

For details, reach out to the publisher.

First published by Grapevine Books, 2025

Copyright © Grapevine, 2025

CONTENTS

PREFACE

The Catholic Church, with more than two thousand years of unbroken tradition, offers one of the richest liturgical experiences in all of Christianity. At the heart of this life of worship is the Holy Mass, a sacred celebration where heaven and earth meet, and believers join in offering praise and thanksgiving to God. For many, the Mass is familiar in sound and rhythm, yet mysterious in meaning. Newcomers may be unsure when to stand, kneel, or respond. Lifelong Catholics may realize they've been reciting the prayers for years without fully understanding their significance.

This guide was created to bridge that gap. Whether you are preparing for the sacraments, returning to the Church after years away, or seeking to deepen your devotion, you will find here a clear, step-by-step companion through every part of the Mass. With explanations, historical background, theological insights, and practical cues for participation, this book will help you enter more fully into the mystery of the Eucharist.

Purpose of This Guide

The purpose of this guide is simple: to help you **understand** and **participate fully** in the Catholic Mass. Too often, the Mass is reduced to a weekly obligation, something attended out of habit rather than embraced as the central act of Christian worship. My hope is that, through these pages, you will see the Mass not as a routine but as a living encounter with Christ Himself.

We will walk through the entire order of the Mass, from the opening procession to the final blessing, showing you what is said, what is done, and why it matters. Every prayer and response of the faithful is included in full, along with explanations of the priest's words and actions. This is not only a "what to say" manual; it is a resource for forming your heart and mind to pray the Mass with reverence and love.

Whether you are in a small rural parish or a grand cathedral, whether the Mass is said in your native language or Latin, this guide will equip you to worship with understanding, confidence, and devotion.

How to Use This Book

This book is meant to be practical. You can read it straight through to build a complete understanding of the Mass, or you can dip into specific sections when you have questions. Each chapter includes:

- **Step-by-step order of the Mass** — showing exactly when each prayer or response occurs.

- **Text in full** — so you can follow along without needing to flip between missals or pew cards.

- **Explanations of meaning** — to deepen your appreciation of the words and actions.

- **Posture and gesture notes** — indicating when to stand, sit, or kneel, and why.

- **Variations** — covering different priestly options, feast day changes, and special rites.

The **Appendices** at the back are designed for quick reference. Appendix E, for example, includes a one-page "Mass Walkthrough Chart" summarizing all words, responses, and gestures in a single visual format, perfect for beginners or for keeping in a pew Bible.

If you are preparing for a special Mass (wedding, funeral, confirmation), refer to Part 3, Chapter 10 for the unique prayers and customs used on those occasions.

Finally, I encourage you not to rush through the explanations. Let the words sink in. The Mass is not only something to understand. It is something to live.

Notes on the Roman Missal

The Roman Missal is the official liturgical book of the Catholic Church that contains the prayers, antiphons, and instructions for celebrating the Mass. The current English translation, implemented in Advent 2011, is faithful to the Latin original while aiming to preserve theological depth and beauty.

The Missal provides both fixed texts — such as the Gloria or Creed, which remain the same from one Mass to another — and variable texts, like the Collect or Preface, which change according to the liturgical season, feast, or occasion. In addition to the spoken words, the Missal contains **rubrics** — printed instructions in red — indicating the actions of the priest, deacon, and congregation.

In this guide, I have followed the structure and wording of the Roman Missal approved for use in the United States (or adapt for your local bishops' conference). Where the priest has more than one approved option for a prayer, those variations are included in full. This ensures that you will be able to follow the Mass confidently no matter which approved Eucharistic Prayer, Penitential Act, or dismissal formula your priest chooses.

Understanding the Missal is key to understanding the Mass, for it holds the Church's official voice of prayer and praise.

Overview: Every Prayer, Response, and Gesture Explained *(200 words)*

This book is organized to take you through the Mass in logical order, with each section building on the last. Part 1 introduces the Mass, its history, and its overall structure. Part 2 walks step-by-step through the actual liturgy, including every word of the prayers and every gesture — from the Sign of the Cross at the start to the bow at the end. Part 3 provides the most common Catholic prayers, as well as guidance for special Masses and occasions. Part 4 explores the deeper spiritual meaning of the Eucharist and shows you how to bring the grace of the Mass into daily life.

Postures are clearly marked: when to stand, sit, kneel, bow, or make the Sign of the Cross. Rubrics and optional variations are explained so you understand the choices the priest may make. With these tools, you will never have to guess what to say or do. Instead, you will be free to pray with focus and devotion, entering into the heart of the Church's worship with confidence and reverence.

PART 1

The Mass Explained – 4,000 words

Chapter 1 – What Is the Catholic Mass? *(1,300 words)*

The Catholic Mass is the central act of worship for the Church and the most important expression of Catholic faith. It is far more than a gathering for prayer or a commemorative meal. In the Mass, the Church participates in the eternal worship of heaven, offering praise, thanksgiving, and sacrifice to God through Jesus Christ in the power of the Holy Spirit. It is the place where the faithful encounter Christ most profoundly, both in His Word and in His Body and Blood.

From the earliest days of Christianity, believers have gathered on the first day of the week to celebrate the Eucharist, obeying Christ's command to "do this in memory of me." This act is both deeply personal and profoundly communal. Each participant offers his or her own prayers, intentions, and thanksgiving, while at the same time joining the entire Church throughout the world in one unified act of worship.

Understanding what the Mass truly is transforms the way we participate in it. It becomes not a routine obligation but a living encounter with God. By exploring its meaning as worship, sacrifice, and celebration, we discover why the Mass is called the "source and summit" of the Christian life.

Worship, Sacrifice, and Celebration

The Mass is first of all worship. Worship means giving God the honor, reverence, and adoration that He alone deserves. It is a response to His infinite goodness and love, and it involves the whole person — mind, heart, and body. In the Mass, worship takes the form of prayers, hymns, responses, and gestures that unite us with the angels and saints in praising the Most Holy Trinity. This worship is directed to God the Father, offered through the Son, and brought to completion in the Holy Spirit.

The Mass is also sacrifice. At its heart is the re-presentation of the one perfect sacrifice of Jesus Christ on the Cross. The Church does not repeat His sacrifice, but makes it present sacramentally in every Mass. The priest, acting in the person of Christ, offers the Body and Blood of the Lord to the Father for the salvation of the world. This is the fulfillment of the Old Testament sacrifices, which foreshadowed the perfect offering of the Lamb of God. When we participate in the Mass, we are united with Christ's self-offering, joining our own prayers, works, joys, and sufferings to His.

This sacrificial aspect is inseparable from the Eucharist itself. At the Last Supper, Jesus instituted this sacrament as both a memorial of His Passion and a means of giving us His very self. By commanding His apostles to "do this in memory of me," He entrusted the Church with the ongoing celebration of this mystery until He comes again.

Yet the Mass is not only solemn sacrifice. It is also a celebration, a sacred banquet in which the faithful receive the very life of God. The altar is both the place of sacrifice and the table of the Lord's Supper, where He feeds His people with His Body and Blood. This dual reality of sacrifice and meal reflects the joy of God's people, who have been redeemed and are invited to share in the heavenly wedding feast of the Lamb.

The celebratory dimension of the Mass is woven into the rhythm of the Church's liturgical year. Each season, Advent, Christmas, Lent, Easter, and Ordinary Time, shapes the prayers, readings, and hymns, inviting us to enter more deeply into the mysteries of Christ's life. Music, vestments, incense, and processions are not mere embellishments; they express the joy, beauty, and reverence of a community gathered in the presence of its Lord.

When we understand the Mass as worship, sacrifice, and celebration, we begin to see that it is not something we attend passively, but something we offer and live. It is the place where heaven and earth meet, where the saving work of Christ is made present, and where we are drawn into the eternal praise of God.

The Real Presence of Christ

At the very heart of the Catholic Mass is the mystery of the Real Presence of Jesus Christ in the Eucharist. This doctrine teaches that, during the consecration at Mass, the bread and wine truly become the Body and Blood, Soul and Divinity of Christ. While the appearances of bread and wine remain, their substance is entirely changed. This change is called transubstantiation, a term defined by the Church to express the depth of this mystery.

The belief in the Real Presence is rooted in the words of Jesus Himself. At the Last Supper, He took bread and said, "This is my Body," and over the chalice He declared, "This is my Blood of the covenant, which will be poured out for many for the forgiveness of sins" (Matthew 26:26–28). These are not symbolic statements. Jesus did not say, "This represents my body" or "This is a reminder of my blood." His words are clear and direct.

In John 6, Jesus expands on this truth, declaring, "My flesh is true food, and my blood is true drink." When some of His listeners found this difficult and began to walk away, He did not call them back with a softer interpretation. Instead, He let them go, confirming the literal meaning of His words. The early Church took this teaching seriously, as shown in the writings of saints and martyrs who risked their lives to receive and protect the Eucharist.

The Church teaches that Christ is present in many ways: in the assembly of the faithful, in the Word proclaimed, in the person of the priest, and in the sacraments. But His presence in the Eucharist is unique because it is the presence of Christ Himself, whole and entire, under the appearances of bread and wine. This is why the Eucharist is called the "source and summit" of the Christian life.

Because of the Real Presence, the Church approaches the Eucharist with the deepest reverence. Catholics genuflect toward the tabernacle, recognizing Christ dwelling there. The consecrated Host is reserved for adoration, carried to the sick, and honored with processions during feasts like Corpus Christi. Eucharistic Adoration allows the faithful to spend time before Christ in prayer, often in silence, contemplating His love and drawing strength from His presence.

The Real Presence also calls the faithful to prepare themselves spiritually before receiving Communion. The Church teaches that one should be in a state of grace, having confessed any grave sins, and should fast for at least one hour before receiving. This preparation expresses our respect for the One we are about to welcome into our hearts.

When we receive the Eucharist, we are not only remembering an event from the past; we are encountering the living Christ here and now. He comes to us personally, uniting us to Himself and to the entire Body of Christ. The more we understand and believe in the Real Presence, the more fully we can participate in the Mass, receiving the Lord with faith, love, and gratitude. In this encounter, our lives are transformed, and we are sent forth to bring His presence into the world.

Chapter 2 – A Brief History of the Mass

The Catholic Mass has a history stretching back two thousand years, rooted in the life of Jesus and the earliest Christian communities. It has developed in form and language over the centuries, yet its core reality has never changed. The same sacrifice of Christ on the Cross, made present under the signs of bread and wine, is offered in every Mass, whether celebrated in a grand cathedral, a small parish, or a humble mission chapel.

Knowing the history of the Mass helps us to appreciate its depth and beauty. The prayers, readings, and gestures are not random or modern inventions. They are the fruit of generations of faith, preserved and handed down by the Church. By tracing its journey from the Upper Room to our present-day liturgy, we see how the Mass has been shaped by culture, language, and the guidance of the Holy Spirit, while remaining faithful to Christ's command to "do this in memory of me."

This history is not just about the past. It shows that the Mass is a living tradition, connecting us to the Apostles, the saints, and all who have worshiped before us, and guiding us toward the eternal banquet in heaven.

From the Last Supper to Today

The Mass began on the night before Jesus suffered and died. During the Passover meal with His Apostles, He took bread, blessed it, broke it, and gave it to them, saying, "This is my Body." He then took a chalice of wine, gave thanks, and said, "This is my Blood of the covenant, which will be poured out for many for the forgiveness of sins." He instructed them to "do this in memory of me" (Luke 22:19). In that moment, Jesus instituted the Eucharist and entrusted it to the Church as the central act of worship.

After the Resurrection and Ascension, the Apostles and early Christians faithfully carried out this command. They gathered on the first day of the week, Sunday, to celebrate the breaking of bread, as described in Acts 2:42. This worship included readings from Scripture, preaching, prayers, and the Eucharistic meal. The structure was simple, but the essentials were already present: the proclamation of the Word and the celebration of the Eucharist.

By the second century, early Christian writers like St. Justin Martyr described the order of worship in a way strikingly similar to today's Mass: readings from the prophets and the apostles, a homily, intercessions, the presentation of bread and wine, prayers of thanksgiving, the consecration, and Communion. The language used depended on the region, with Greek being common in the East and Latin gradually taking hold in the West.

As Christianity spread, the Eucharist moved from private homes to larger assembly halls and eventually to dedicated church buildings. By the fourth century, after Emperor Constantine legalized Christianity, public worship flourished. The use of Latin became standard in the Western Church, and the liturgy grew more structured. Over time, prayers were fixed, ceremonial actions became more elaborate, and sacred music and vestments developed to reflect the dignity of the celebration.

The medieval period brought even greater uniformity, culminating in the reforms of the Council of Trent in the sixteenth century. The Tridentine Mass, celebrated in Latin according to the Roman Missal of 1570, became the norm for the Catholic world. This form of the Mass emphasized solemnity, precision, and reverence, with the priest often praying quietly at the altar while the faithful followed along in personal missals or in silent prayer.

The twentieth century saw a renewed emphasis on active participation by the faithful, leading to the liturgical reforms of the Second Vatican Council (1962–1965). The Council called for the restoration of certain ancient practices, a wider use of Scripture in the readings, and the option to celebrate Mass in local languages. The revised form of the Mass, known as the Novus Ordo, was promulgated in 1970. It retained the same essential structure but expanded the variety of prayers and Scripture passages, encouraged responses from the congregation, and allowed the priest to face the people during the liturgy.

Today, both the Novus Ordo and the Traditional Latin Mass are celebrated in the Church. Despite differences in language, form, and ceremonial detail, both are the same Eucharistic sacrifice, offered to the glory of God and for the sanctification of His people. The history of the Mass shows how the Church, guided by the Holy Spirit, has preserved the heart of Christ's gift while adapting its expression to the needs of the faithful in every age.

Latin Mass and Novus Ordo Overview

The **Latin Mass**, often referred to as the Traditional Latin Mass or the Tridentine Mass, is the form of the Roman Rite codified after the Council of Trent in the sixteenth century and celebrated according to the Roman Missal of 1962. It is conducted entirely in Latin, the official liturgical language of the Church in the West, with the exception of the homily and certain announcements. In this form, the priest faces the altar in the same direction as the congregation, a posture known as *ad orientem*, symbolizing the community facing God together in worship. The prayers and readings follow a fixed structure, and the calendar of feasts and seasons is distinct from the newer form. Silence, reverence, and precise ceremonial actions are hallmarks of the Traditional Latin Mass, and its beauty has drawn generations of Catholics to deep devotion.

The **Novus Ordo Mass**, or Ordinary Form of the Roman Rite, was introduced in 1970 following the reforms of the Second Vatican Council. While it can be celebrated in Latin, it is most often offered in the local vernacular. The structure remains rooted in the same four main parts of the Mass, but there is greater flexibility in the choice of prayers, readings, and music. The priest may face the people (*versus populum*) or the altar, and the expanded lectionary provides a richer selection of Scripture over a three-year Sunday cycle and a two-year weekday cycle. The Novus Ordo emphasizes active participation by the congregation through spoken responses, singing, and other forms of engagement.

Both forms are fully valid and share the same essence: the one sacrifice of Christ made present on the altar. The Church treasures them as two expressions of the same mystery, each offering its own way of drawing the faithful into the worship of God.

Chapter 3 – The Four Main Parts

The Catholic Mass is rich in prayers, symbols, and rituals, but it follows a clear and purposeful structure. This structure is divided into four main parts, each with a distinct focus that draws the faithful deeper into the mystery of Christ's saving work. These parts are the **Introductory Rites**, the **Liturgy of the Word**, the **Liturgy of the Eucharist**, and the **Concluding Rites**. Understanding these sections helps us follow the flow of the liturgy and participate more fully, knowing the meaning and purpose behind every word and action.

The Mass begins with the Introductory Rites, which gather the community and prepare hearts to hear the Word of God and to celebrate the Eucharist. The Liturgy of the Word then proclaims the Scriptures and offers an opportunity to respond in faith. In the Liturgy of the Eucharist, we enter into the sacrifice of Christ, offering ourselves with Him and receiving His Body and Blood. Finally, the Concluding Rites send us forth to live what we have celebrated.

By seeing the Mass as a unified whole made up of these interconnected parts, we come to realize that every gesture, every prayer, and every response is part of one great act of worship offered to God.

Introductory Rites

The Introductory Rites open the celebration of the Mass and serve an important purpose: they bring the faithful together into one worshiping community, help them prepare their hearts and minds, and set the spiritual tone for the entire liturgy. These opening moments are not simply a formality before the "main" part of the Mass. They are a sacred preparation that draws us from the ordinary rhythms of life into the extraordinary reality of worshiping God in the Eucharist.

The Introductory Rites begin with the Entrance Procession. This is more than a practical way for the ministers to reach the altar; it is a symbolic act that represents the Church on pilgrimage toward the heavenly kingdom. The cross leads the way, followed by servers, lectors, and other ministers, with the priest as the shepherd of the assembly. If incense is used, it rises as a sign of our prayers ascending to God. A hymn or chant often accompanies the procession, chosen to reflect the liturgical season or the feast being celebrated.

Upon reaching the sanctuary, the ministers bow or genuflect according to the placement of the tabernacle, and the priest kisses the altar. This kiss is an act of reverence to Christ, whom the altar represents, and it recalls the tradition of venerating the relics of saints contained within many altars.

The priest then leads the congregation in the Sign of the Cross, invoking the name of the Father, the Son, and the Holy Spirit. This gesture marks the Mass as a Trinitarian act of worship and reminds us of our baptism, through which we became children of God.

The Greeting follows, with the priest using words from Scripture such as "The Lord be with you." The people respond, "And with your spirit," recognizing the presence of Christ in the priest's ministry. This exchange is not a casual hello but a liturgical acknowledgment that all present are gathered in the presence of the Lord.

The Penitential Act comes next, offering the faithful an opportunity to acknowledge their sins and seek God's mercy. This may take the form of the Confiteor, a communal prayer of confession, or brief invocations followed by "Lord, have mercy" or "Christ, have mercy." On certain days, the Kyrie is sung or recited, an ancient cry for mercy that has been part of Christian worship for centuries.

On Sundays outside of Advent and Lent, the Gloria follows the Penitential Act. This joyful hymn of praise, rooted in the words of the angels at the birth of Christ, gives glory to God and sets a tone of celebration. It is addressed to the Father, the Son, and the Holy Spirit, proclaiming God's greatness and His work of salvation.

The Introductory Rites conclude with the Collect. In this prayer, the priest invites the people to pray, pauses for silent intentions, and then offers a prayer that gathers together the needs and hopes of the assembly. The Collect varies according to the liturgical day and introduces the theme of the Mass.

By the end of the Introductory Rites, the community has moved from individual prayer into a united act of worship, hearts have been lifted to God, and the assembly is ready to listen attentively to His Word in the Liturgy of the Word.

Liturgy of the Word

The Liturgy of the Word is the portion of the Mass in which God speaks to His people through Sacred Scripture. It is rooted in the ancient tradition of synagogue worship, where readings from the Law and the Prophets were proclaimed and explained. In the Mass, this proclamation is enriched by the presence of Christ, who is the Word made flesh.

The First Reading is typically drawn from the Old Testament, except during the Easter season when it comes from the Acts of the Apostles. This reading recalls God's saving works and prepares us to see how they are fulfilled in Christ. The congregation responds with the Responsorial Psalm, a prayer taken from the Book of Psalms, either sung or recited, with verses and a repeated refrain.

The Second Reading, found on Sundays and solemnities, is taken from the New Testament letters or the Book of Revelation. These writings encourage and instruct the Church in living out the Gospel.

Before the Gospel, the congregation stands to sing the Alleluia or another seasonal acclamation, welcoming Christ who speaks to us. The Gospel is then proclaimed by the deacon or priest, and it contains the very words and actions of the Lord.

After the Gospel, the homily explains the readings and applies them to daily life. On Sundays and solemnities, the Profession of Faith follows, in which the Church proclaims her beliefs in the Nicene or Apostles' Creed. The Liturgy of the Word concludes with the Prayer of the Faithful, where petitions are offered for the Church, the world, and those in need, allowing the faithful to respond to the Word with prayer.

Liturgy of the Eucharist

The Liturgy of the Eucharist is the heart of the Mass. In it, the sacrifice of Christ on the Cross is made present, and the faithful are invited to unite themselves with His offering and receive Him in Holy Communion.

It begins with the Presentation of the Gifts, in which bread and wine, along with other offerings, are brought to the altar. These gifts symbolize the work of human hands and the lives of the faithful offered to God. The priest prepares the altar, prays over the offerings, and invites the people to join in prayer that God will accept the sacrifice.

The Eucharistic Prayer follows. This is the central prayer of the Mass, beginning with the Preface and the Sanctus ("Holy, Holy, Holy"). At the heart of this prayer is the consecration, when, through the power of the Holy Spirit and the words of Christ, the bread and wine truly become His Body and Blood. The priest elevates the consecrated Host and Chalice for adoration, and the congregation responds with faith and reverence.

The Eucharistic Prayer concludes with the Doxology and the Great Amen, after which the faithful pray the Lord's Prayer together. The Sign of Peace is then shared, symbolizing unity and reconciliation. The Lamb of God is sung as the Host is broken, and the faithful come forward to receive Holy Communion. After a moment of silent prayer or song, the priest prays the Prayer after Communion, giving thanks for the grace received in the sacrament.

Concluding Rites

The Concluding Rites bring the celebration of the Mass to a close and send the faithful forth to live the Gospel in their daily lives. Although brief compared to the earlier parts of the liturgy, these rites are significant because they remind the congregation that the grace received in the Eucharist is not meant to remain within the church walls. Instead, it is meant to transform hearts and actions in the world.

The Concluding Rites typically begin with any necessary announcements. These may include parish news, upcoming events, or pastoral reminders. While not strictly part of the liturgy, announcements are placed here so they do not interrupt the flow of the Mass earlier. They are practical in nature but should be delivered briefly and with respect for the sacred setting.

Following the announcements, the priest invites the people to receive the Final Blessing. This blessing is a prayer asking God to protect, guide, and strengthen the faithful as they go forth. Depending on the liturgical season or the nature of the celebration, the blessing may be simple or more solemn. On special occasions, a more elaborate blessing with multiple invocations may be used. The faithful make the Sign of the Cross as the blessing is imparted, receiving it as a gift of grace.

After the blessing, the dismissal is given. If a deacon is present, he proclaims it; otherwise, the priest does so. The words of dismissal vary: "Go forth, the Mass is ended," "Go and announce the Gospel of the Lord," "Go in peace, glorifying the Lord by your life," or simply "Go in peace." Each of these formulas emphasizes mission. The Mass does not end in the sense of worship being completed; rather, it sends the Church into the world to continue worship through service, witness, and holy living.

The people respond, "Thanks be to God," affirming their willingness to live out the Gospel message they have heard and the grace they have received. This response is not simply polite; it is an expression of gratitude for the gift of the Mass and a joyful acceptance of the call to discipleship.

A recessional hymn or chant often accompanies the priest and ministers as they process out of the church. Like the Entrance Procession, this movement is symbolic. The ministers, having led the assembly in worship, now lead the people out into the mission field of the world. The congregation may remain standing until the procession has left the church, after which many pause in personal prayer before departing.

The Concluding Rites may seem simple, but they carry a deep message. They remind us that the Eucharist is both a gift to be received and a mission to be lived. Having been nourished by Christ's Body and Blood, the faithful are called to be His presence to others, to bring the peace, mercy, and love of God into homes, workplaces, schools, and communities. In this way, the liturgy continues in everyday life, and the worship offered at the altar bears fruit in the world.

The Mass truly sends us forth as living witnesses of the Kingdom of God, ready to serve, to proclaim, and to love as Christ has loved us.

PART 2

The Order of the Mass – 13,000 words

Chapter 4 – Introductory Rites

The Introductory Rites mark the beginning of the Mass and set the tone for the sacred celebration that follows. They are designed to gather the faithful into a unified community, prepare hearts and minds for worship, and focus attention on God. In these opening moments, the Church transitions from the busyness of daily life to the solemnity and joy of the liturgy.

Every gesture, prayer, and response in the Introductory Rites has meaning. The entrance hymn or chant reminds us that we are pilgrims on a journey toward our heavenly home. The greeting from the priest affirms the presence of Christ in the midst of the assembly. The Penitential Act calls us to acknowledge our sins and seek God's mercy so that we may celebrate the sacred mysteries with pure hearts.

This section of the Mass is not just a formality before the "main" parts. It is an essential preparation, helping each person to enter fully into the mystery of the Eucharist. When approached with understanding and reverence, the Introductory Rites open the door to a deeper encounter with God, readying us to hear His Word and to share in the sacrifice of Christ.

Entrance Procession and Greeting

The Mass begins with the Entrance Procession, a solemn movement that brings the ministers into the sanctuary and sets the spiritual tone for the entire celebration. Though outwardly simple, this procession is rich in meaning and symbolism. It reminds the faithful that the Church is a pilgrim people, always journeying toward God, and that every liturgy is part of the greater pilgrimage of life leading to the heavenly kingdom.

The procession typically starts at the rear of the church, with altar servers, lectors, and extraordinary ministers of Holy Communion forming an ordered line. If a crucifer is present, the cross is carried high, leading the assembly as Christ leads His people. This visible symbol of the Lord's Passion and victory is the central focus of the entrance. When incense is used, the thurifer swings the censer rhythmically, the rising smoke symbolizing prayers ascending to heaven. In larger celebrations, candle bearers flank the cross or the Book of the Gospels, emphasizing the light of Christ and the Word of God.

The Entrance Chant or hymn accompanies the procession, chosen to suit the liturgical day or season. Its purpose is to foster unity, introduce the theme of the Mass, and accompany the entrance of the priest and ministers. The General Instruction of the Roman Missal notes that this chant may be drawn from the antiphons provided in the Missal or from a suitable hymn. When sung by the entire congregation, it is a powerful expression of unity in prayer.

Upon reaching the sanctuary, the ministers bow profoundly to the altar. If the tabernacle is located directly behind the altar, they genuflect instead. The priest and deacon then approach the altar itself. The altar is not just a table but a sacred symbol of Christ, the cornerstone of the Church and the place where His sacrifice will be made present. For this reason, the priest reverently kisses the altar, sometimes joined by the deacon, as a sign of veneration and devotion. When incense is used, the priest incenses the altar, circling it with deliberate motions, showing honor to Christ and to the relics of saints often placed within the altar stone.

After venerating the altar, the priest proceeds to the chair, from where he will lead the Introductory Rites. Once the hymn concludes, the assembly begins the Mass with the Sign of the Cross. The priest, extending his hand, says, "In the name of the Father, and of the Son, and of the Holy Spirit," to which the people respond, "Amen." This ancient gesture recalls baptism and marks everything that follows as a Trinitarian act of worship.

The priest then greets the assembly with words taken from Scripture. The most common greeting is, "The Lord be with you," and the faithful respond, "And with your spirit." Other approved greetings may be used, such as "The grace of our Lord Jesus Christ, and the love of God, and the communion of the Holy Spirit be with you all." These greetings are not casual acknowledgments but solemn affirmations of God's presence within His Church. By responding, the faithful acknowledge the Spirit of God at work in the priest, who acts in the person of Christ.

At this moment, the assembly is fully gathered, united as one body, and ready to begin the sacred mysteries. The Entrance Procession and Greeting remind everyone present that they are part of something greater than themselves, a community drawn together by Christ to worship the Father in the Spirit. What began as individuals arriving from many directions now becomes one Church, standing together in God's presence.

Penitential Act (Confiteor, Kyrie)

After the Greeting, the Mass moves into the Penitential Act, a moment of collective humility before God. Its purpose is to prepare the faithful to celebrate the sacred mysteries with purified hearts. This rite is not a substitute for sacramental confession, but it does cleanse venial sins and helps dispose the faithful to receive the Eucharist with reverence.

There are three main forms of the Penitential Act approved by the Roman Missal. The first and perhaps most familiar is the **Confiteor**, which begins with the words, "I confess to almighty God." In this prayer, each person acknowledges personal sinfulness not only before God but also before "you, my brothers and sisters." This communal dimension highlights that sin is never purely private; it affects the whole Body of Christ. The faithful strike their breasts at the words "through my fault, through my fault, through my most grievous fault," a gesture of contrition and sincerity. The prayer concludes by asking for the intercession of the Blessed Virgin Mary, the angels, and the saints, as well as the prayers of the entire community.

The second form consists of short invocations, often called tropes, each followed by the response "Lord, have mercy" or "Christ, have mercy." These invocations highlight different aspects of Christ's saving work, such as healing the sick, forgiving sinners, or interceding for His people. This form is simple, adaptable, and emphasizes the mercy of Christ in concrete ways.

The third form is the **Kyrie eleison** itself, which means "Lord, have mercy" in Greek. It may be used on its own or as part of the other forms. The Kyrie is one of the most ancient prayers of the liturgy, dating back to the early Church when Greek was the common language of prayer. Its repetition fosters a spirit of repentance and reliance on God's mercy.

After the Penitential Act, the priest pronounces the absolution: "May almighty God have mercy on us, forgive us our sins, and bring us to everlasting life." The people respond, "Amen." Although this is not sacramental absolution, it is a real assurance of God's mercy and a fitting preparation for the celebration of the Eucharist.

Gloria and Collect

On most Sundays of the year, as well as on solemnities and feasts, the Gloria follows the Penitential Act. This hymn of praise begins with the angelic song at the birth of Christ: "Glory to God in the highest, and on earth peace to people of good will." It is a joyful outpouring of worship that shifts the tone from repentance to celebration.

The Gloria is addressed to all three Persons of the Trinity. It glorifies God the Father, acknowledges Jesus Christ as the Son of God and Redeemer, and honors the Holy Spirit. The hymn emphasizes both God's majesty and His mercy, recalling that Christ "takes away the sins of the world" and sits at the right hand of the Father as our intercessor. Because of its exalted nature, the Gloria is typically sung, although it may be recited when music is not possible.

Following the Gloria, the priest introduces the **Collect**, also known as the Opening Prayer. The Collect gathers the silent prayers of the faithful into one concise petition addressed to God. Its structure usually includes an invocation of God, a reference to His saving works, a request for a particular grace, and a conclusion through Christ in the Holy Spirit. The Collect varies by liturgical day, reflecting the season or feast being celebrated.

When the priest says, "Let us pray," he pauses briefly in silence, allowing the congregation to call to mind personal intentions. Then he prays the Collect on behalf of the entire assembly, and the people affirm the prayer with a strong "Amen." With this, the Introductory Rites are brought to their conclusion. The faithful, having confessed their sins, praised God's glory, and united their intentions, are now spiritually prepared to listen to the Word of God in the Liturgy of the Word.

Gestures and Movements of Priest, Deacon, and Ministers

The liturgy of the Mass is a dialogue of both words and actions. The gestures and movements of the priest, deacon, and other ministers are not incidental but integral to the meaning of the celebration. Each movement communicates reverence, unity, and the sacred mystery of what is taking place. When performed with care, these actions elevate the liturgy, helping the faithful recognize the presence of Christ. When neglected, the sense of reverence can be diminished. For this reason, every gesture has significance and purpose.

The Priest

The priest is the principal celebrant of the Mass. His gestures reflect his role as one who stands in the person of Christ the Head. Upon entering the sanctuary, the priest bows profoundly to the altar or genuflects if the Blessed Sacrament is present nearby. He then kisses the altar as a sign of veneration for Christ, the living stone. In some celebrations, incense is used, and the priest incenses the altar, making deliberate movements that express honor to Christ and the saints whose relics may be placed within the altar.

During the Penitential Act, the priest may bow slightly to express humility before God.

At the prayers addressed to God on behalf of the people, he extends his hands in the orans posture, symbolizing his role as mediator. At the Gospel, if no deacon is present, the priest signs the book of the Gospels with the Sign of the Cross and traces small crosses on his forehead, lips, and chest.

The most solemn gestures of the priest occur during the Eucharistic Prayer. He places his hands over the bread and wine during the epiclesis, invoking the Holy Spirit. At the words of consecration, he bows slightly and speaks with clarity and reverence. He then elevates the Host and Chalice so the faithful may adore Christ present under the sacramental signs. Following each elevation, the priest genuflects in adoration. These gestures are central moments of the liturgy, inviting the whole congregation into profound reverence.

Before Communion, the priest shows the consecrated Host to the assembly, saying, "Behold the Lamb of God." His movement here is not only functional but theological: he holds Christ before His people, inviting them to see with the eyes of faith. At the end of Mass, he extends his hands over the people in blessing and makes the Sign of the Cross to send them forth in peace.

The Deacon

When present, the deacon has a distinctive role expressed in both words and actions. In the Entrance Procession, the deacon may carry the Book of the Gospels high before him. This gesture symbolizes the centrality of God's Word in the life of the Church. Upon reaching the altar, the deacon places the book on it and, with the priest, kisses the altar.

At the proclamation of the Gospel, the deacon bows before the priest and quietly asks for a blessing. He then processes to the ambo carrying the Book of the Gospels, preceded by candles and sometimes incense. Before proclaiming, he makes the Sign of the Cross on his forehead, lips, and heart, modeling what the people also do. After proclaiming, he kisses the book and says quietly, "Through the words of the Gospel may our sins be wiped away."

In the Liturgy of the Eucharist, the deacon prepares the altar, pours the wine and water into the chalice, and assists the priest. He also helps distribute Communion and carefully purifies the vessels afterward. At the conclusion of the Mass, the deacon dismisses the congregation with words such as, "Go in peace" or "Go and announce the Gospel of the Lord." His gestures and words are direct and mission-focused, reminding the faithful of their call to bring Christ into the world.

Altar Servers

Altar servers assist the priest and deacon by carrying the cross, candles, incense, and other items needed for the liturgy. In the Entrance Procession, the cross is held high, serving as a focal point for the assembly. Candles are carried to honor the altar, the Gospel, and the Eucharist. Servers bow or genuflect at the appropriate times, modeling reverence for the congregation.

When holding the missal for the priest, presenting the cruets, or bringing the lavabo for the washing of hands, servers are expected to move with steadiness and attentiveness. Their actions, though simple, contribute to the dignity of the celebration. The quiet discipline of altar servers communicates that the Mass is sacred and worthy of careful attention.

Lectors

Lectors approach the ambo with composure and reverence. Before ascending, they bow toward the altar, acknowledging its significance. Their proclamation of Scripture is itself a gesture, for the Word of God is not merely read but proclaimed to the assembly. After completing the reading, the lector pauses briefly, then returns to their place with the same calm reverence.

Extraordinary Ministers of Holy Communion

Extraordinary ministers of Holy Communion assist in distributing the Eucharist when needed. Their gestures begin with a bow toward the altar before approaching to receive the sacred vessels. When distributing, they hold the Host or chalice reverently, looking at the communicant as they say the prescribed words, "The Body of Christ" or "The Blood of Christ." Their movements must be careful and deliberate, reflecting belief in the Real Presence. After distribution, they return the vessels and bow in reverence before resuming their places.

Postures and Common Gestures

The entire assembly joins the ministers in shared gestures that express unity in worship. Standing is the posture of respect and readiness, used during the Gospel, prayers, and hymns. Sitting is a posture of attentive listening, especially during the readings and homily. Kneeling is the posture of adoration, most notably during the consecration.

Bows and genuflections are key gestures of reverence. A bow of the head is made at the name of Jesus, Mary, or the saint of the day. A deeper bow from the waist is given to the altar or during the Creed at the words of the Incarnation. Genuflection, dropping to one knee, is reserved for the Blessed Sacrament and for the cross on Good Friday.

The Sign of the Cross is one of the most familiar gestures, made at the beginning and end of Mass, before and after the Gospel, and at other moments. It is both a personal and communal sign of belonging to Christ.

The Harmony of Gestures

What unites all of these actions is harmony. The movements of priest, deacon, and ministers are carried out with purpose and reverence, creating a rhythm that guides the congregation into worship. When performed with care, they elevate the liturgy and draw attention to the sacred mysteries rather than to the individuals performing them.

Gestures and movements in the Mass are not performance or decoration. They are signs of faith expressed in the body. Together with the prayers and readings, they form one act of worship in which the whole Church, on earth and in heaven, offers glory to God.

Chapter 5 – Liturgy of the Word

The Liturgy of the Word is the first major portion of the Mass after the Introductory Rites. In this sacred moment, God speaks directly to His people through the proclamation of Sacred Scripture. What begins as written words on a page becomes the living Word of God when proclaimed aloud in the midst of the assembly. Here, the faithful listen, reflect, and respond, just as Israel once listened to the Law and the Prophets and as the first Christians gathered to hear the Apostles' teaching.

This part of the Mass is more than a series of readings. It is a dialogue between God and His people. God speaks in the Scriptures, the homily explains and applies His Word, and the congregation responds with prayer, profession of faith, and intercession. The Liturgy of the Word nourishes the mind and heart, preparing the faithful to enter into the Eucharistic sacrifice with deeper understanding and devotion.

The structure of the Liturgy of the Word — readings, psalms, Gospel, homily, Creed, and intercessions — mirrors the pattern of salvation history: God reveals His plan, calls His people to faith, and invites them into covenant relationship. It is both instruction and encounter, drawing the Church into living communion with Christ, the Word made flesh.

First Reading (Example Readings and Psalm Refrains)

The First Reading of the Mass introduces the faithful to the Word of God and provides the foundation for the themes that unfold throughout the rest of the liturgy. On Sundays and solemnities, this reading is usually taken from the Old Testament, though during the Easter season it comes from the Acts of the Apostles. The First Reading connects the people of God with the history of salvation, reminding us that the covenantal love revealed in Scripture is fulfilled in Christ and continues in the Church today.

The proclamation of the First Reading is never to be thought of as simply "storytelling." It is God Himself who speaks to His people through human words. For this reason, the lector approaches the ambo with reverence, bows to the altar before ascending, and proclaims the reading with clarity and solemnity. The conclusion of the reading, "The Word of the Lord," is met by the congregation's response, "Thanks be to God." This dialogue makes clear that the faithful not only hear the Scriptures but receive them as God's living Word.

The choice of First Readings follows the Church's lectionary cycle. Sundays follow a three-year cycle (Years A, B, and C), and weekdays follow a two-year cycle (Years I and II). This cycle ensures that across several years the faithful hear a broad and rich portion of the Scriptures.

Example of a First Reading

From the Book of Isaiah (Isaiah 9:1–2, 5–6):

"The people who walked in darkness have seen a great light; upon those who lived in a land of gloom a light has shone. You have brought them abundant joy and great rejoicing, as they rejoice before you as at the harvest, as people make merry when dividing spoils. For a child is born to us, a son is given us; upon his shoulder dominion rests. They name him Wonder-Counselor, God-Hero, Father-Forever, Prince of Peace."

This passage is read at the Christmas Mass during the Night, foreshadowing the coming of Christ as the light of the world.

Another example comes from the Book of Exodus (Exodus 16:2–4, 12–15):

"The whole congregation of the children of Israel grumbled against Moses and Aaron in the desert. The Lord said to Moses, 'I will now rain down bread from heaven for you. Each day the people are to go out and gather their daily portion. I have heard the grumbling of the children of Israel. Tell them: In the evening twilight you shall eat flesh, and in the morning you shall have your fill of bread, so that you may know that I, the

Lord, am your God.'"

This reading prefigures the gift of the Eucharist, the true bread from heaven.

Psalm Refrains

After the First Reading, the assembly responds with the Responsorial Psalm, which is either sung or recited. The psalms are prayers inspired by the Holy Spirit, and they give the people a way to reflect on what they have just heard. Each psalm is arranged with a refrain that the congregation repeats, often between verses sung by a cantor. The refrain allows everyone to participate and makes the psalm a prayer of the whole community.

Examples of common psalm refrains include:

- "The Lord is my shepherd; there is nothing I shall want." (Psalm 23)

- "Let us go rejoicing to the house of the Lord." (Psalm 122)

- "Taste and see the goodness of the Lord." (Psalm 34)

- "Lord, let your mercy be on us, as we place our trust in you." (Psalm 33)

- "If today you hear his voice, harden not your hearts." (Psalm 95)

The Responsorial Psalm is important because it bridges the First Reading and the Gospel, often echoing themes of God's mercy, covenant love, or saving power. The repetition of the refrain impresses these truths on the hearts of the faithful, allowing Scripture to become prayer.

Through the First Reading and Psalm, the faithful are reminded of God's constant presence throughout salvation history. They learn that the same God who spoke to Israel continues to speak today and that the stories of old are not distant history but part of the unfolding plan of salvation that reaches its fullness in Christ.

Responsorial Psalm and Gospel Acclamation

After the First Reading, the assembly responds with the Responsorial Psalm. This moment is not only a bridge between the readings but also a time of prayer. The psalms are inspired songs given to Israel and now to the Church, filled with expressions of praise, thanksgiving, lament, and trust. When the psalm is prayed in the liturgy, it becomes the voice of the Church speaking to God and at the same time God speaking through His Word to His people.

The Responsorial Psalm is usually sung, with a cantor or choir leading the verses and the congregation joining in the refrain. Singing allows the psalms to be prayed with greater depth, since they were originally composed as sacred songs. If singing is not possible, the psalm may be recited, but the structure of alternating verses and refrain remains. The refrain is repeated several times, helping the faithful to take its words into their hearts. For example, during Easter the refrain might be "This is the day the Lord has made; let us rejoice and be glad." In Lent, it might be "Be merciful, O Lord, for we have sinned." Each refrain connects closely with the theme of the readings and the season.

The Responsorial Psalm is followed by the Gospel Acclamation. On most days, this is the joyful cry of "Alleluia," a Hebrew word meaning "Praise the Lord." The Alleluia is often repeated by the whole assembly, with a verse of Scripture sung by the cantor in between. This verse usually relates directly to the Gospel that is about to be proclaimed. During Lent, when the Alleluia is set aside as a sign of penitence, another acclamation such as "Praise to you, Lord Jesus Christ, King of endless glory" is used.

The purpose of the Gospel Acclamation is to prepare the assembly to hear Christ Himself speak in the Gospel. It is not a mere transition but an act of praise that honors Christ's presence in His Word. The congregation stands during the Alleluia, a posture of readiness and respect, and sings with full voice. Candles may be carried to the ambo, and incense may be used to mark the solemnity of the moment.

Together, the Responsorial Psalm and the Gospel Acclamation serve as a dialogue of love between God and His people. The psalm allows the Church to reflect on God's deeds and respond in faith, while the Alleluia invites the faithful to welcome Christ who is about to speak. In these chants, the assembly learns to listen, to rejoice, and to prepare their hearts for the Gospel, the high point of the Liturgy of the Word.

Gospel Reading (Dialogue and Postures)

The proclamation of the Gospel is the high point of the Liturgy of the Word. While the other readings are also inspired Scripture, the Gospel is accorded special honor because it records the words and deeds of the Lord Jesus Christ Himself. The gestures, postures, and dialogue surrounding the Gospel reflect its central importance and invite the faithful to listen with reverence and openness.

The Gospel is usually proclaimed by a deacon, or by the priest when no deacon is present. Before approaching the ambo, the deacon or priest bows before the celebrant and quietly asks for a blessing. The celebrant prays, "May the Lord be in your heart and on your lips, that you may proclaim His Gospel worthily and well." If incense is used, the minister carries the Book of the Gospels in procession, flanked by candles to emphasize the light of Christ.

The congregation stands for the Gospel as a sign of respect and readiness to receive the Lord's teaching. The minister begins with the greeting, "The Lord be with you," and the people respond, "And with your spirit." He then announces, "A reading from the holy Gospel according to [Matthew, Mark, Luke, or John]." At this moment, all trace the small Sign of the Cross on their forehead, lips, and chest, silently praying that God's Word may be in their mind, on their lips, and in their heart.

If incense is used, the book is incensed before the proclamation. The Gospel is then read solemnly and clearly, often chanted on major feasts to highlight its dignity. The words of the Gospel are not explained here; the proclamation itself is the event of Christ speaking to His Church.

At the conclusion, the minister proclaims, "The Gospel of the Lord," and the people respond, "Praise to you, Lord Jesus Christ." The book may then be kissed by the minister as a sign of veneration. On special occasions, it may also be shown to the congregation or used to bless them.

The posture of standing throughout the Gospel proclaims the people's attentiveness and honor. The signing of the forehead, lips, and heart reminds them to think about, speak about, and treasure the Gospel. The candles, incense, and acclamations add solemnity and joy. All of these actions, combined with the dialogue between minister and people, highlight that this is not just a reading but an encounter with the living Word of God, Jesus Christ.

In this moment, the Church listens to the voice of the Good Shepherd. The faithful are not passive spectators but active listeners who receive His Word, preparing to carry it into their daily lives.

Homily

Following the proclamation of the Gospel, the priest or deacon delivers the homily. The purpose of the homily is to explain the Scriptures, connect them to the mysteries being celebrated, and apply them to the lives of the faithful. It is not a lecture or personal reflection, but a continuation of the dialogue between God and His people begun in the readings.

The homily should illuminate the Word of God, helping the congregation understand its meaning in the context of salvation history and its relevance for Christian living today. It may draw connections between the Old Testament and the Gospel, explain the teachings of Christ, or offer guidance on how to live out the faith in everyday life.

On Sundays and holy days of obligation, the homily is required, though it is strongly recommended at all Masses. The Church considers the homily an essential part of nourishing the faith of the community. When delivered with prayer and clarity, it strengthens belief, fosters devotion, and inspires action. The homily concludes the proclamation of the Word, preparing the faithful to respond in faith and prayer.

Profession of Faith (Nicene Creed, Apostles' Creed)

After the homily on Sundays and solemnities, the congregation recites the Profession of Faith. This act is more than a recitation of words. It is a communal declaration of belief, a summary of the truths of the faith handed down from the Apostles. By proclaiming the Creed, the faithful renew their baptismal promises and affirm their unity with the universal Church.

The Nicene Creed, developed by the Councils of Nicaea and Constantinople, is the form most often used at Mass. It begins with "I believe in one God" and affirms belief in the Father, Son, and Holy Spirit. It emphasizes the divinity of Christ, His Incarnation, Passion, Resurrection, and Ascension, as well as the role of the Holy Spirit and the unity of the Church. During the Creed, the faithful bow at the words, "and by the Holy Spirit was incarnate of the Virgin Mary, and became man." On Christmas and the Annunciation, they genuflect at these words to honor the mystery of the Incarnation.

The Apostles' Creed, an older and simpler formula of faith, may be used especially in Masses with children or during Lent and Easter. It reflects the faith professed by the early Church, beginning with "I believe in God, the Father almighty."

Reciting the Creed together strengthens the bond of the faithful as one people professing one faith. It also serves as a transition from hearing the Word of God to offering prayers and sacrifice at the altar. The Creed is a reminder that participation in the Eucharist is not only an act of worship but also an act of faith, uniting believers in the truths revealed by Christ and safeguarded by the Church.

Chapter 5 – Liturgy of the Eucharist

The Liturgy of the Eucharist is the heart of the Mass. In this part of the celebration, the Church obeys Christ's command at the Last Supper: "Do this in memory of me." What began as a simple meal with the Apostles becomes, through the power of the Holy Spirit, the sacramental re-presentation of Christ's sacrifice on the Cross. Here, the faithful are invited to unite themselves with Christ's perfect offering to the Father and to be nourished by His Body and Blood in Holy Communion.

This portion of the Mass begins with the Presentation of the Gifts, in which bread and wine are brought to the altar. The priest offers prayers over these gifts, which symbolize both the work of human hands and the lives of the faithful offered to God. The central prayer of the Church, the Eucharistic Prayer, follows. In it, the priest invokes the Holy Spirit, recounts salvation history, and speaks the words of Christ that bring about the consecration.

The Liturgy of the Eucharist culminates in Communion, where the faithful receive Christ Himself under the forms of bread and wine. This sacred banquet both unites the Church to her Lord and strengthens her for the mission of living out the Gospel.

Presentation of the Gifts and Altar Preparation

The Presentation of the Gifts begins the Liturgy of the Eucharist. It is sometimes referred to as the Offertory, because it is the moment when the bread and wine are offered to God in preparation for the sacrifice of the Mass. What may appear simple on the surface carries deep symbolic meaning. In this act, the Church presents not only bread and wine but also the prayers, works, and sacrifices of the faithful. These gifts will soon become the Body and Blood of Christ, but before that transformation they represent the offering of the community and their participation in the saving mystery.

The gifts are usually brought forward in a procession by members of the congregation. This procession has its roots in the early Church, when the faithful would bring bread, wine, oil, and other goods to support the clergy and the poor. Today, the procession retains its symbolic power, showing that the whole Church is offering something to God. The bread and wine are received by the priest or deacon and placed upon the altar. Sometimes other gifts for the needs of the Church or for the poor are also presented, reminding us that love of neighbor is inseparable from worship of God.

Once the gifts are placed on the altar, the priest offers prayers of blessing over them. Lifting the paten with the bread, he says quietly or aloud, "Blessed are you, Lord God of all creation, for through your goodness we have received the bread we offer you." Similar words are prayed over the chalice of wine. These prayers echo Jewish table blessings, reminding us of the continuity between the Last Supper and the Eucharist. The people often respond with "Blessed be God forever," uniting their voices with the priest's prayer.

The priest then adds a small amount of water to the wine in the chalice. This action has multiple layers of meaning. Practically, it recalls the mixture of water and wine used in ancient meals. Symbolically, it represents the union of Christ with His Church, the divine and human natures joined together in the Incarnation, and the blood and water that flowed from Christ's side on the Cross. As he mixes the water and wine, the priest prays quietly, "By the mystery of this water and wine may we come to share in the divinity of

Christ who humbled himself to share in our humanity."

After preparing the chalice, the priest bows profoundly and prays silently that he may be cleansed from sin to offer the sacrifice worthily. If incense is used, the priest may then incense the gifts on the altar, the altar itself, and the cross, showing reverence for Christ who will soon be present in the sacrament. The deacon or another minister may incense the priest and the people, a reminder that the entire assembly is part of the offering.

The priest then washes his hands at the side of the altar in a ritual known as the lavabo. As water is poured over his fingers, he prays quietly, "Wash me, O Lord, from my iniquity and cleanse me from my sin." This act is a practical purification but also a spiritual one, symbolizing the priest's desire to be made pure before handling the sacred mysteries.

After these preparations, the priest invites the people to pray: "Pray, brothers and sisters, that my sacrifice and yours may be acceptable to God, the almighty Father." The congregation stands and responds, "May the Lord accept the sacrifice at your hands for the praise and glory of his name, for our good and the good of all his holy Church." This exchange emphasizes that the offering of bread and wine, which will soon become Christ's sacrifice, belongs to the whole community, not only to the priest.

Finally, the priest prays the Prayer over the Offerings, which varies depending on the day or season. This prayer asks God to accept the gifts and prepare the Church to share in the Eucharistic mystery. With the altar prepared and the gifts presented, the community is ready to enter into the central prayer of the Mass, the Eucharistic Prayer.

In the Presentation of the Gifts, the faithful see their own lives symbolically placed on the altar. Their prayers, joys, sufferings, and labors are united with the bread and wine, soon to be transformed into the Body and Blood of Christ. This moment teaches that the Mass is not only the work of the priest but the prayer of the whole Church, offered for the glory of God and the salvation of the world.

Consecration and Elevation of the Host and Chalice

The consecration is the most solemn moment of the Mass, the point at which the bread and wine become the Body and Blood of Christ. This is not a mere symbol or remembrance, but the sacramental re-presentation of the one sacrifice of Calvary. The Church teaches that, through the words of Christ spoken by the priest and the power of the Holy Spirit, the bread and wine are transubstantiated. Their outward appearances remain, but their substance is changed entirely into Christ Himself.

The priest begins with the words of institution, recounting what Jesus did at the Last Supper. Taking the bread into his hands, he gives thanks and speaks the words of Christ: "This is my Body, which will be given up for you." At this very moment, the bread is consecrated. The priest then elevates the Host above the altar, showing it to the people so that they may adore Christ now truly present. This elevation is often accompanied by the ringing of bells, a custom that emphasizes the sacredness of the moment and alerts even those at a distance to the miracle taking place. After the elevation, the priest places the Host back on the paten and genuflects in adoration.

The consecration of the wine follows in the same solemn manner. The priest takes the chalice, gives thanks, and pronounces Christ's words: "This is the chalice of my Blood, the Blood of the new and eternal covenant, which will be poured out for you and for many for the forgiveness of sins. Do this in memory of me." At these words, the wine is changed into the Blood of Christ. The priest then elevates the chalice, again showing it to the faithful, who may quietly pray an act of faith and adoration such as "My Lord and my God." The chalice is then placed back on the altar, and the priest genuflects once more.

These gestures are not only signs of reverence by the priest but invitations to the entire congregation to recognize the profound mystery before them. The act of elevation is meant to draw the eyes and hearts of the faithful upward, reminding them that heaven touches earth at this moment. Many respond interiorly with prayer, offering their own lives in union with the sacrifice of Christ now made present.

The consecration and elevation are surrounded by silence, broken only by the priest's words and perhaps the sound of bells. This silence is itself an act of worship, a recognition that human speech cannot fully capture the holiness of the event. The faithful are encouraged to bow their heads, kneel in adoration, or silently affirm their belief in Christ's real presence.

Theologically, these moments highlight both the sacrificial and the communal aspects of the Eucharist. The Body given up and the Blood poured out recall the Cross, yet the elevation also points to the gift offered to the whole Church, uniting heaven and earth. The faithful are not passive observers but participants, uniting their prayers with the offering of Christ to the Father.

In every Mass, the consecration and elevation proclaim that Christ is truly present — Body, Blood, Soul, and Divinity. This presence invites adoration, thanksgiving, and faith. It is the heart of Catholic worship, the moment when the eternal sacrifice of Christ is made present to the Church in a way that transcends time and space, nourishing His people and renewing the covenant of love between God and humanity.

The Lord's Prayer

Following the consecration and the memorial prayers, the liturgy turns to the Lord's Prayer, also known as the *Our Father*. This prayer, given by Jesus Himself to His disciples, is the perfect model of Christian prayer. In the Mass, it is not prayed privately but as the prayer of the entire Church gathered around the altar.

The priest introduces the prayer with an invitation, reminding the faithful that they dare to call God "Our Father" because of the Spirit received in baptism. The entire congregation then recites or sings the words together: "Our Father, who art in heaven..." This communal recitation emphasizes that the Eucharist is celebrated not by individuals alone but by the whole Body of Christ united in worship.

After the Lord's Prayer, the priest prays the embolism: "Deliver us, Lord, we pray, from every evil..." This prayer expands on the final petition of the Our Father, asking for peace, protection from sin, and freedom from distress as the Church awaits the return of Christ in glory. The people conclude with the acclamation, "For the kingdom, the power, and the glory are yours, now and forever." This dialogue sets the tone of hope and confidence in God's providence.

Sign of Peace and Lamb of God

The liturgy then continues with the Rite of Peace. The priest prays, "Lord Jesus Christ, who said to your Apostles, 'Peace I leave you, my peace I give you,' look not on our sins, but on the faith of your Church…" This prayer recalls Christ's gift of peace to His disciples after the Resurrection, a peace rooted in reconciliation with God. The priest asks that the Church be granted unity and peace in accordance with God's will.

After this, the priest greets the people: "The peace of the Lord be with you always," and they respond, "And with your spirit." Then, if appropriate, the deacon or priest invites the congregation to offer one another a sign of peace. This gesture, often a handshake, bow, or other culturally suitable sign, expresses reconciliation and communion among the faithful before they approach the altar to receive the Body and Blood of Christ. It is a reminder that unity with Christ in the Eucharist must also mean unity with our brothers and sisters.

As the exchange of peace concludes, the liturgy moves into the *Agnus Dei* or "Lamb of God." While the priest breaks the consecrated Host, the assembly sings or says: "Lamb of God, you take away the sins of the world, have mercy on us… grant us peace." The fraction rite, in which the Host is broken, recalls Christ's body broken for us on the Cross, while the invocation acknowledges Him as the Lamb of God who takes away the sins of the world.

The repeated plea for mercy and peace during the *Agnus Dei* prepares the faithful to approach Communion with humility and reverence. The action of breaking the bread also highlights the communal dimension of the Eucharist: though many receive, all share in the one Bread of Life. Together, the Sign of Peace and the Lamb of God form a bridge between the Eucharistic Prayer and the reception of Holy Communion, fostering a spirit of reconciliation, humility, and awe before the presence of Christ.

Communion Rite (Gestures, Posture, Receiving the Eucharist)

The Communion Rite is the culmination of the Liturgy of the Eucharist. After the consecration, the prayers, and the Sign of Peace, the faithful are invited to receive the Body and Blood of Christ in Holy Communion. This sacred moment unites each person with Christ Himself and deepens the bond of unity within the Church. Because of its significance, the Communion Rite is surrounded by gestures and postures that express reverence and devotion.

The rite begins with the **Fraction**, in which the priest breaks the consecrated Host. This action recalls how Christ's Body was broken for us on the Cross. The priest may place a small piece of the Host into the chalice, a sign of the unity of Christ's Body and Blood in the sacrifice. During this time, the congregation prays or sings the *Agnus Dei*, repeatedly calling on Christ, the Lamb of God, to have mercy and grant peace. This litany helps prepare the faithful to receive Communion with humility.

Following this, the priest elevates the Host above the paten or the chalice and proclaims: "Behold the Lamb of God, behold Him who takes away the sins of the world. Blessed are those called to the supper of the Lamb." The faithful respond with the prayer of the centurion: "Lord, I am not worthy that you should enter under my roof, but only say the word and my soul shall be healed." This response acknowledges our unworthiness yet expresses confidence in Christ's saving power.

The faithful then come forward to receive Holy Communion. The Church prescribes a posture of reverence as each communicant approaches. In many places, the norm is to bow the head before receiving. Depending on the region and permission of the bishops' conference, Communion may be received either on the tongue or in the hand.

In both cases, the communicant responds "Amen" after the minister says, "The Body of Christ," affirming faith in the Real Presence. When receiving in the hand, the host should be placed immediately into the mouth in front of the minister to avoid any risk of profanation. When receiving on the tongue, the communicant tilts the head slightly back and opens the mouth so that the minister can place the Host reverently.

If the chalice is offered, the minister presents it, saying, "The Blood of Christ." The communicant responds "Amen" and drinks a small amount before carefully returning the chalice. This sharing in both species highlights the fullness of the Eucharistic banquet, although the Church teaches that Christ is fully present under each form.

Throughout the distribution of Communion, the posture of the faithful is one of reverence. The universal norm is standing, though in some countries kneeling is permitted or customary. Silence is encouraged, though hymns of thanksgiving and adoration may also accompany the reception. The most important element is an interior attitude of prayer, gratitude, and awareness that one is receiving Christ Himself.

After Communion, the faithful return to their seats and spend time in silent thanksgiving. This personal prayer is vital, allowing each person to enter into intimate dialogue with Christ present within them. Some may recite traditional prayers of thanksgiving, while others may simply sit in quiet adoration. The priest also prays silently after Communion before returning to the chair and leading the Prayer after Communion, which concludes the rite.

The gestures and postures of the Communion Rite — bowing, standing or kneeling, responding "Amen," receiving with care, and silent prayer — are all outward signs of the faith of the Church. They remind the faithful that the Eucharist is not ordinary bread and wine but the true Body and Blood of Christ. This sacred food strengthens the soul, forgives venial sins, and deepens union with the Lord and with the whole Church.

In receiving Communion, the faithful enter into the mystery of Christ's sacrifice and are nourished with divine life. It is the moment when the promise of Jesus — "He who eats my flesh and drinks my blood has eternal life" — is fulfilled in a real and personal way. The Communion Rite is therefore both a solemn act of worship and a joyful encounter with Christ, drawing the Church into closer communion with Him and with one another.

Communion Rite (Gestures, Posture, Receiving the Eucharist)

The Communion Rite is the culmination of the Liturgy of the Eucharist. After the consecration, the prayers, and the Sign of Peace, the faithful are invited to receive the Body and Blood of Christ in Holy Communion. This sacred moment unites each person with Christ Himself and deepens the bond of unity within the Church. Because of its significance, the Communion Rite is surrounded by gestures and postures that express reverence and devotion.

The rite begins with the **Fraction**, in which the priest breaks the consecrated Host. This action recalls how Christ's Body was broken for us on the Cross. The priest may place a small piece of the Host into the chalice, a sign of the unity of Christ's Body and Blood in the sacrifice. During this time, the congregation prays or sings the *Agnus Dei*, repeatedly calling on Christ, the Lamb of God, to have mercy and grant peace. This litany helps prepare the faithful to receive Communion with humility.

Following this, the priest elevates the Host above the paten or the chalice and proclaims:

"Behold the Lamb of God, behold Him who takes away the sins of the world. Blessed are those called to the supper of the Lamb." The faithful respond with the prayer of the centurion: "Lord, I am not worthy that you should enter under my roof, but only say the word and my soul shall be healed." This response acknowledges our unworthiness yet expresses confidence in Christ's saving power.

The faithful then come forward to receive Holy Communion. The Church prescribes a posture of reverence as each communicant approaches. In many places, the norm is to bow the head before receiving. Depending on the region and permission of the bishops' conference, Communion may be received either on the tongue or in the hand. In both cases, the communicant responds "Amen" after the minister says, "The Body of Christ," affirming faith in the Real Presence. When receiving in the hand, the host should be placed immediately into the mouth in front of the minister to avoid any risk of profanation. When receiving on the tongue, the communicant tilts the head slightly back and opens the mouth so that the minister can place the Host reverently.

If the chalice is offered, the minister presents it, saying, "The Blood of Christ." The communicant responds "Amen" and drinks a small amount before carefully returning the chalice. This sharing in both species highlights the fullness of the Eucharistic banquet, although the Church teaches that Christ is fully present under each form.

Throughout the distribution of Communion, the posture of the faithful is one of reverence. The universal norm is standing, though in some countries kneeling is permitted or customary. Silence is encouraged, though hymns of thanksgiving and adoration may also accompany the reception. The most important element is an interior attitude of prayer, gratitude, and awareness that one is receiving Christ Himself.

After Communion, the faithful return to their seats and spend time in silent thanksgiving. This personal prayer is vital, allowing each person to enter into intimate dialogue with Christ present within them. Some may recite traditional prayers of thanksgiving, while others may simply sit in quiet adoration. The priest also prays silently after Communion before returning to the chair and leading the Prayer after Communion, which concludes the rite.

The gestures and postures of the Communion Rite — bowing, standing or kneeling, responding "Amen," receiving with care, and silent prayer — are all outward signs of the faith of the Church. They remind the faithful that the Eucharist is not ordinary bread and wine but the true Body and Blood of Christ. This sacred food strengthens the soul, forgives venial sins, and deepens union with the Lord and with the whole Church.

In receiving Communion, the faithful enter into the mystery of Christ's sacrifice and are nourished with divine life. It is the moment when the promise of Jesus — "He who eats my flesh and drinks my blood has eternal life" — is fulfilled in a real and personal way. The Communion Rite is therefore both a solemn act of worship and a joyful encounter with Christ, drawing the Church into closer communion with Him and with one another.

Chapter 6: Eucharistic Prayer

Eucharistic Prayer I (The Roman Canon)

Eucharistic Prayer I, known as the Roman Canon, is the oldest and most venerable of the Eucharistic Prayers in the Roman Rite. Its roots stretch back to the first centuries of the Church, and by the sixth century, its essential form was already established. For well over 1,000 years, the Roman Canon was the only Eucharistic Prayer used in the Latin Church. This long history gives it a unique place of honor.

The Roman Canon was codified after the Council of Trent in the Missal of Pope Pius V (1570) and remained virtually unchanged until the Second Vatican Council. When Pope Paul VI introduced the revised Missal in 1970, three new Eucharistic Prayers were added, but the Roman Canon was preserved as Eucharistic Prayer I. Today, it is often chosen for solemnities, feast days of Apostles and Martyrs, and other major celebrations because of its rich and formal tone.

Theological Themes

The Roman Canon emphasizes the sacrificial nature of the Mass more strongly than the other prayers. It repeatedly refers to the offering of Christ to the Father and unites this offering with the sacrifices of the Church. Its language is reverent and precise, underscoring the holiness of the mystery being celebrated.

Another distinctive theme is communion with the saints. The Roman Canon contains long lists of Apostles and early Martyrs, invoking their intercession. This practice highlights the unity of the Church on earth with the Church in heaven.

The Canon also includes prayers for both the living and the dead. This reflects the Catholic belief that the Eucharist is offered for the entire Church: for those present, for those who have gone before, and for those still to come.

Structure Overview

The Roman Canon follows a clear structure:

1. **Preface and Sanctus** – Praises God for His works and joins the angels in the hymn "Holy, Holy, Holy."

2. **Prayers for the Church and the Pope and Bishop** – Asking God to guard and guide the Church.

3. **Commemoration of the Living** – Prayers for specific individuals and all gathered.

4. **Invocation of the Saints (Communicantes)** – Calling upon Mary, Joseph, the Apostles, and a list of early Martyrs.

5. **Prayer over the Offerings (Hanc Igitur)** – Asking God to accept the sacrifice of His family, the Church.

6. **Consecration** – The heart of the prayer, when the bread and wine become the Body and Blood of Christ.

7. **Offering of Christ (Unde et Memores)** – The priest offers Christ's Body and Blood to the Father.

8. **Commemoration of the Dead (Memento etiam)** – Remembering those who have died and asking God to grant them rest.

9. **Second Invocation of Saints (Nobis quoque peccatoribus)** – Acknowledging our

own sinfulness and asking to share in the company of the saints.

10. **Doxology** – Giving glory to the Father through Christ, concluded with the Great Amen.

Gestures and Postures

The Roman Canon is accompanied by distinctive gestures that express reverence. The priest bows during certain prayers, extends his hands over the gifts during the epiclesis, and makes the Sign of the Cross multiple times over the offerings. At the words of consecration, he bows slightly, then elevates the Host and Chalice for adoration, followed by genuflections in reverence.

The faithful kneel throughout the Eucharistic Prayer, a posture of adoration and humility. They stand again after the Great Amen, ready to pray the Lord's Prayer.

Why It Matters

The Roman Canon holds a special place in the Roman Rite because it links the Church today with the earliest generations of Christians. Its language, rich in solemnity, emphasizes the Mass as true sacrifice. Its invocation of the saints reminds us that we never worship alone; we are always surrounded by the "great cloud of witnesses." Its prayers for the living and the dead show that the Eucharist unites the whole Church across time and space.

For these reasons, the Roman Canon is often chosen for solemn occasions. It is a prayer that calls us to awe, reverence, and thanksgiving as we stand at the foot of the Cross and share in the eternal sacrifice of Christ.

Eucharistic Prayer I (Roman Canon)

Section 1: Introductory Dialogue and Preface

Latin Text with Rubrics

Sacerdos:

Dominus vobiscum.

Populus:

Et cum spiritu tuo.

Sacerdos:

Sursum corda.

Populus:

Habemus ad Dominum.

Sacerdos:

Gratias agamus Domino Deo nostro.

Populus:

Dignum et iustum est.

(Then the priest continues with the Preface, appropriate to the season or feast. The Preface always ends with the Sanctus.)

Omnes (cum sacerdote):

Sanctus, Sanctus, Sanctus Dominus Deus Sabaoth.

Pleni sunt caeli et terra gloria tua.

Hosanna in excelsis.

Benedictus qui venit in nomine Domini.

Hosanna in excelsis.

Explanatory Summary (English)

The Eucharistic Prayer begins with a solemn dialogue between the priest and the congregation. These words are among the oldest in Christian worship, preserved since the earliest centuries.

● The priest greets the people: "The Lord be with you," and the people respond: "And with your spirit." This acknowledges the presence of Christ in the priest, who will soon act in His person.

● The priest invites the people to lift up their hearts. They respond that their hearts are already lifted to the Lord, symbolizing readiness for prayer.

● Finally, the priest calls the people to give thanks to God, and they affirm: "It is right and just."

This dialogue leads into the Preface, which varies depending on the liturgical season or the specific feast being celebrated. The Preface praises God for His works of creation, redemption, and sanctification, and always concludes by joining our voices with the angels in the great hymn of the **Sanctus** ("Holy, Holy, Holy").

The Sanctus, taken from Isaiah 6 and the Gospel accounts of Christ's entry into Jerusalem, is sung or said by the whole assembly. It expresses both awe before the holiness of God and joy at the coming of Christ, who enters sacramentally upon the altar as He once entered the Holy City. At this moment, the whole Church joins heaven in proclaiming God's glory.

Section 2: The Canon Part I

*(Prayers for the Church and Living: **Te igitur, Memento Domine, Communicantes**)*

Latin Text with Rubrics

Sacerdos, extensis manibus:

Te igitur, clementissime Pater,

per Iesum Christum, Filium tuum, Dominum nostrum,

supplices rogamus ac petimus,

uti accepta habeas et benedicas

haec dona, haec munera, haec sancta sacrificia illibata,

in primis, quae tibi offerimus pro Ecclesia tua sancta catholica:

quam pacificare, custodire, adunare et regere digneris

toto orbe terrarum,

una cum famulo tuo Papa nostro N.

et Antistite nostro N.,

et omnibus orthodoxis atque catholicae et apostolicae fidei cultoribus.

(Pause briefly for the Church and its leaders.)

Memento Domine,

famulorum famularumque tuarum N. et N.

(Here the priest joins his hands and prays silently for those living whom he wishes to remember, then extends hands again and continues aloud.)

et omnium circumstantium,

quorum tibi fides cognita est et nota devotio,

pro quibus tibi offerimus:

vel qui tibi offerunt hoc sacrificium laudis,

pro se, suisque omnibus:

pro redemptione animarum suarum,

pro spe salutis et incolumitatis suae:

tibique reddunt vota sua aeterno Deo, vivo et vero.

Communicantes,

et memoriam venerantes,

in primis gloriosae semper Virginis Mariae, Genetricis Dei

et Domini nostri Iesu Christi:

sed et beati Ioseph, eiusdem Virginis Sponsi,

et beatorum Apostolorum ac Martyrum tuorum,

Petri et Pauli, Andreae,

(Iacobi, Ioannis, Thomae, Iacobi, Philippi, Bartholomaei, Matthaei, Simonis et Thaddaei:

Lini, Cleti, Clementis, Xysti, Cornelii, Cypriani, Laurentii, Chrysogoni,

Ioannis et Pauli, Cosmae et Damiani)

et omnium Sanctorum tuorum;

quorum meritis precibusque concedas,

ut in omnibus protectionis tuae muniamur auxilio.

Per Christum Dominum nostrum. Amen.

Explanatory Summary (English)

This first part of the Canon is focused on **prayers for the Church and the living**, and on establishing communion with the saints.

1. Te igitur (We therefore beseech you)

- The priest begins the Canon by addressing God the Father, through Jesus Christ, offering the gifts of bread and wine and asking Him to accept them.

- Special prayers are made for the **universal Church**, asking God to grant her peace, unity, and protection.

- The priest mentions the **Pope** and the **local Bishop by name**, showing that every Mass is celebrated in union with the Church's leaders, a visible sign of Catholic unity.

2. Memento Domine (Remember, O Lord)

- Here the priest prays for the **living**, naming specific people silently in his heart. This personal moment connects the sacrifice of the Mass to the needs of individuals.

- The prayer then expands to all present at the Mass and for their families, intentions, and hopes. The faithful are reminded that they bring their lives, prayers, and concerns to God at the altar.

3. Communicantes (In communion with)

- This prayer establishes communion with the **Blessed Virgin Mary, St. Joseph, the Apostles, and early martyrs**. The long list of names is deliberate: it roots the Church's worship in continuity with those who first witnessed to Christ, even at the cost of their lives.

- By invoking these saints, the priest acknowledges that the Mass is never celebrated by the earthly congregation alone, but always in union with the heavenly Church.

- The prayer ends with the request that, through the intercession of the saints, God may protect the faithful in all things.

These prayers highlight three essential dimensions of the Mass: it is a prayer for the **whole Church**, a prayer offered for the **living faithful and their intentions**, and a prayer celebrated in **communion with the saints of heaven**. The Mass is not an isolated act but a participation in the living, universal Body of Christ.

Section 3: The Canon Part II

*(Prayer over the Offerings and Consecration: **Hanc igitur**, **Quam oblationem**, Institution Narrative)*

Latin Text with Rubrics

Sacerdos, extensis manibus:

Hanc igitur oblationem servitutis nostrae,

sed et cunctae familiae tuae, quaesumus, Domine,

ut placatus accipias:

diesque nostros in tua pace disponas,

atque ab aeterna damnatione nos eripi

et in electorum tuorum iubeas grege numerari.

Per Christum Dominum nostrum. Amen.

Sacerdos, manibus extensis super oblata:

Quam oblationem tu, Deus, in omnibus, quaesumus,

benedictam, adsriptam, ratam, rationabilem, acceptabilemque facere digneris:

ut nobis Corpus et Sanguis fiat dilectissimi Filii tui, Domini nostri Iesu Christi.

Institution of the Eucharist

Qui pridie quam pateretur,

accipit panem in sanctas ac venerabiles manus suas,

et elevatis oculis in caelum ad te Deum, Patrem suum omnipotentem,

tibi gratias agens, benedixit, fregit,

deditque discipulis suis, dicens:

Accipite et manducate ex hoc omnes:

hoc est enim Corpus meum,

quod pro vobis tradetur.

(He shows the consecrated Host to the people, places it on the paten, and genuflects in adoration.)

Simili modo, postquam cenatum est,

accipiens et hunc praeclarum calicem

in sanctas ac venerabiles manus suas:

item tibi gratias agens, benedixit,

deditque discipulis suis, dicens:

Accipite et bibite ex eo omnes:

hic est enim calix Sanguinis mei,

novi et aeterni testamenti:

mysterium fidei:

qui pro vobis et pro multis effundetur

in remissionem peccatorum.

Hoc facite in meam commemorationem.

(He shows the chalice to the people, places it on the corporal, and genuflects in adoration.)

Explanatory Summary (English)

1. Hanc igitur (Therefore, Lord, we pray)

- This prayer asks God to accept the Church's offering of bread and wine.

- The priest prays that God will order our days in His peace, deliver us from eternal damnation, and count us among the elect. This shows that the Eucharist is not just about ritual but about salvation and eternal life.

2. Quam oblationem (Be pleased, O God, we pray)

- The priest extends his hands over the gifts, invoking the Holy Spirit in a gesture of blessing.

- He asks God to make the offering holy, spiritual, and acceptable, that it may become the Body and Blood of Christ. This anticipates the consecration and makes clear that the transformation is God's work, not human.

3. Institution Narrative and Consecration

- At this moment, the priest recalls the actions of Jesus at the Last Supper. Using the very words of Christ, he consecrates the bread and wine.

- The faithful kneel in adoration. The priest elevates the Host and the Chalice so that the people may worship Christ truly present. Each elevation is followed by a genuflection of the priest in reverence.

- The words "This is my Body" and "This is the chalice of my Blood" mark the heart of the Eucharistic Prayer, when transubstantiation takes place and Christ is sacramentally present on the altar.

This section is the most sacred part of the Canon. It unites the Church with Christ's sacrifice on Calvary, making His offering present to us in a real and unbloody manner. Every word, gesture, and silence is full of reverence, reminding us that heaven and earth meet at this moment on the altar.

Section 4: The Canon Part III

*(Offering of Christ and Commemoration of the Dead: **Unde et memores**, **Supra quae**, **Supplices te rogamus**, **Memento etiam**)

Latin Text with Rubrics

Unde et memores, Domine,

nos servi tui, sed et plebs tua sancta,

eiusdem Christi Filii tui Domini nostri,

tam beatae passionis,

necnon et ab inferis resurrectionis,

sed et in caelos gloriosae ascensionis:

offerimus praeclarae maiestati tuae

de tuis donis ac datis

Hostiam puram, Hostiam sanctam, Hostiam immaculatam,

Panem sanctum vitae aeternae,

et Calicem salutis perpetuae.

Supra quae propitio ac sereno vultu respicere digneris:

et accepta habere, sicuti accepta habere dignatus es

munera pueri tui iusti Abel,

et sacrificium patriarchae nostri Abrahae,

et quod tibi obtulit summus sacerdos tuus Melchisedech,

sanctum sacrificium, immaculatam hostiam.

Supplices te rogamus, omnipotens Deus:

iube haec perferri per manus sancti Angeli tui

in sublime altare tuum,

in conspectu divinae maiestatis tuae:

ut, quotquot ex hac altaris participatione

sacrosanctum Filii tui Corpus et Sanguinem sumpserimus,

omni benedictione caelesti et gratia repleamur.

Per Christum Dominum nostrum. Amen.

Memento etiam, Domine,

famulorum famularumque tuarum N. et N.,

qui nos praecesserunt cum signo fidei,

et dormiunt in somno pacis.

(The priest joins his hands and prays silently for the dead, then continues aloud:)

Ipsis, Domine, et omnibus in Christo quiescentibus,

locum refrigerii, lucis et pacis,

ut indulgeas, deprecamur.

Per Christum Dominum nostrum. Amen.

Explanatory Summary (English)

1.   Unde et memores (Therefore, O Lord, as we celebrate the memorial)

● The priest recalls the Passion, Resurrection, and Ascension of Christ.

● He offers to God the Father the pure, holy, and spotless victim: Christ Himself present in the Eucharist.

● The bread and wine, now consecrated, are described as the holy Bread of eternal life and the Chalice of everlasting salvation.

2.   Supra quae (Be pleased to look upon these offerings)

● The priest asks God to accept the sacrifice just as He accepted the gifts of Abel, the sacrifice of Abraham, and the offering of Melchizedek.

● This links the Eucharist to the history of salvation, showing it as the fulfillment of all earlier sacrifices.

3.   Supplices te rogamus (In humble prayer we ask you)

● The priest bows deeply while praying that God will command His holy Angel to carry this sacrifice to the heavenly altar before the throne of divine majesty.

- This prayer expresses the connection between the earthly altar and the heavenly liturgy.

- It also asks that all who receive the Body and Blood of Christ may be filled with every grace and blessing.

4. Memento etiam (Remember also, Lord)

- Here the priest prays for the dead. He pauses to remember by name those who have died, then asks God to grant them a place of refreshment, light, and peace.

- The prayer emphasizes that the Eucharist is offered for the salvation of both the living and the departed.

This section of the Roman Canon highlights the sacrificial dimension of the Mass. The offering is no longer bread and wine but Christ Himself, offered in an unbloody manner to the Father. It also emphasizes the communion of the Church across time: we pray for those who have died, trusting that the merits of Christ's sacrifice extend beyond the grave.

Section 5: The Canon Part IV

*(Invocation of Saints, Doxology, and the Great Amen: **Nobis quoque peccatoribus, Per quem haec omnia, Per ipsum**)*

Latin Text with Rubrics

Nobis quoque peccatoribus,

famulis tuis, de multitudine miserationum tuarum sperantibus,

partem aliquam et societatem donare digneris,

cum tuis sanctis Apostolis et Martyribus:

cum Ioanne, Stephano, Matthia, Barnaba,

Ignatio, Alexandro, Marcellino, Petro,

Felicitate, Perpetua, Agatha, Lucia,

Agnete, Caecilia, Anastasia,

et omnibus Sanctis tuis:

intra quorum nos consortium non aestimator meriti,

sed veniae, quaesumus, largitor admitte.

Per Christum Dominum nostrum.

Per quem haec omnia, Domine,

semper bona creas,

sanctificas, vivificas, benedicis,

et praestas nobis.

(The priest takes the paten with the Host and the chalice and, raising both slightly, says:)

Per ipsum, et cum ipso, et in ipso,

est tibi Deo Patri omnipotenti,

in unitate Spiritus Sancti,

omnis honor et gloria,

per omnia saecula saeculorum.

Populus:

Amen.

(This Amen, often called the Great Amen, is sung or said by all the people together.)

Explanatory Summary (English)

1. **Nobis quoque peccatoribus (To us also, your servants, who though sinners)**

●   The priest prays for himself and for all the faithful, humbly acknowledging their sinfulness.

●   He asks God to grant them a share in the fellowship of the saints, not because of their merits, but through God's abundant mercy.

●   Another list of saints is invoked here, including John the Baptist, Stephen, Matthias, Barnabas, Ignatius, Alexander, and several early martyrs. This reinforces the deep sense of communion with those who have already triumphed in Christ.

2. **Per quem haec omnia (Through whom you continue to create all these good things)**

●   The priest acknowledges that all creation, sanctification, life, and blessing come through Christ.

●   This prayer ties together the offering of the Eucharist with God's ongoing work of grace in the world.

3. **Per ipsum (Through Him, and with Him, and in Him)**

●   Holding the consecrated Body and Blood of Christ, the priest offers the doxology: a final hymn of glory to God the Father, through Christ, in the unity of the Holy Spirit.

●   This is the climax of the Roman Canon, expressing the Trinitarian nature of Christian worship.

4. The Great Amen

- The people respond with a solemn "Amen," often sung. This Amen is more than a closing word — it is the people's assent to the entire Eucharistic Prayer. In this moment, the offering made by the priest becomes the offering of the whole Church.

- By saying "Amen," the faithful make Christ's sacrifice their own, uniting themselves completely with Him and with His Body, the Church.

Eucharistic Prayer II

Section 1: Summary and Explanation

Eucharistic Prayer II is the shortest of the four main Eucharistic Prayers. It was composed after the Second Vatican Council and is inspired by a very ancient prayer found in the *Apostolic Tradition* attributed to St. Hippolytus of Rome (3rd century). Its language is simpler and more concise than the Roman Canon, making it especially suitable for weekday Masses or for occasions when brevity is needed.

Theological Themes

The prayer emphasizes:

- **God's holiness**: "You are indeed Holy, O Lord, the fount of all holiness."

- **The role of the Holy Spirit**: calling upon the Spirit to sanctify the gifts.

- **The institution narrative**: the words of Christ at the Last Supper.

- **Communion**: asking that those who partake may be gathered into one by the Spirit.

- **Prayer for the Church**: remembrance of the Pope, Bishop, clergy, and all the faithful.

- **Prayers for the dead**: asking God to grant them eternal light and peace.

It is shorter than the Roman Canon, but no less profound, stressing the essentials of the Eucharist in a direct and clear manner.

Structure Overview

1. Preface dialogue and Sanctus (as in all Eucharistic Prayers).

2. Epiclesis: the Holy Spirit is invoked upon the bread and wine.

3. Institution Narrative: words of consecration.

4. Anamnesis: recalling Christ's death and Resurrection.

5. Offering: presenting the Body and Blood of Christ to the Father.

6. Intercessions: prayers for the Church, clergy, living, and dead.

7. Doxology: glory to the Father through Christ in the Spirit, concluding with the Great Amen.

Gestures and Postures

- The priest extends hands over the gifts during the epiclesis.

- The bread and chalice are elevated after the consecration for adoration.

- The faithful kneel during the consecration.

- The prayer concludes with the raising of the chalice and paten at the doxology, with all responding "Amen."

Section 2: Full Latin Text with Rubrics and Commentary

Preface Dialogue and Sanctus

Sacerdos:

Dominus vobiscum.

Populus:

Et cum spiritu tuo.

Sacerdos:

Sursum corda.

Populus:

Habemus ad Dominum.

Sacerdos:

Gratias agamus Domino Deo nostro.

Populus:

Dignum et iustum est.

(Then follows the Preface, proper to the day or season, which ends with the Sanctus.)

Omnes:

Sanctus, Sanctus, Sanctus Dominus Deus Sabaoth.

Pleni sunt caeli et terra gloria tua.

Hosanna in excelsis.

Benedictus qui venit in nomine Domini.

Hosanna in excelsis.

Epiclesis

Sacerdos, extensis manibus super oblata:

Vere Sanctus es, Domine, fons omnis sanctitatis.

Haec ergo dona, quaesumus, Spiritus tui rore sanctifica,

ut nobis Corpus et + Sanguis fiant

Domini nostri Iesu Christi.

(The priest joins his hands and makes the Sign of the Cross once over the bread and chalice.)

Institution Narrative

Qui cum Passioni voluntarie traderetur,

accipiens panem, gratias egit, fregit,

deditque discipulis suis, dicens:

Accipite et manducate ex hoc omnes:

hoc est enim Corpus meum,

quod pro vobis tradetur.

(The priest shows the consecrated Host to the people, places it on the paten, and genuflects in adoration.)

Simili modo, postquam cenatum est,

accipiens calicem, iterum gratias egit,

deditque discipulis suis, dicens:

Accipite et bibite ex eo omnes:

hic est enim calix Sanguinis mei

novi et aeterni testamenti,

qui pro vobis et pro multis effundetur

in remissionem peccatorum.

Hoc facite in meam commemorationem.

(The priest shows the chalice to the people, places it on the corporal, and genuflects in adoration.)

Anamnesis and Offering

Sacerdos:

Memores igitur mortis et resurrectionis eius,

tibi, Domine, panem vitae et calicem salutis offerimus,

gratias agentes quia nos dignos habuisti

astare coram te et tibi ministrare.

Et supplices deprecamur

ut Corporis et Sanguinis Christi participes a Spiritu Sancto congregemur in unum.

Intercessions

Recordare, Domine, Ecclesiae tuae toto orbe diffusa,

ut eam in caritate perficias una cum Papa nostro N.

et Episcopo nostro N.

et universo clero.

Memento etiam fratrum nostrorum,

qui in spe resurrectionis dormierunt,

omniumque in tua miseratione defunctorum,

et eos in lumen vultus tui admitte.

Omnium nostrum, quaesumus, miserere,

ut cum beata Dei Genetrice, Virgine Maria,

beato Ioseph, eius Sponso,

beatis Apostolis et omnibus Sanctis,

qui tibi a saeculo placuerunt,

aeterni vitae mereamur esse consortes,

et te laudemus et glorificemus

per Filium tuum Iesum Christum.

Doxology

Sacerdos, tenens patenam cum Hostia et calicem, dicit:

Per ipsum, et cum ipso, et in ipso,

est tibi Deo Patri omnipotenti,

in unitate Spiritus Sancti,

omnis honor et gloria

per omnia saecula saeculorum.

Populus:

Amen.

Explanatory Commentary (English)

- **Epiclesis:** The priest calls down the Holy Spirit upon the gifts of bread and wine, asking that they become the Body and Blood of Christ. The Sign of the Cross is traced over the offerings.

- **Institution Narrative:** The priest recounts the Last Supper, pronouncing Christ's words over the bread and wine. At this moment, through the power of the Spirit, transubstantiation occurs. The Host and chalice are elevated for adoration, followed by genuflection.

- **Anamnesis and Offering:** The Church remembers Christ's death and resurrection and offers the "bread of life and chalice of salvation" to the Father. The prayer also asks the Spirit to gather all who share the Eucharist into unity.

- **Intercessions:** Prayers are offered for the Church, the Pope, the local Bishop, clergy, the living, and the dead. This shows the Eucharist as prayer for the whole Body of Christ.

- **Communion of Saints:** Mary, Joseph, the Apostles, and all the saints are invoked as companions in eternal life.

- **Doxology and Great Amen:** The prayer concludes by glorifying the Father through Christ in the unity of the Spirit. The "Amen" of the people makes the entire Eucharistic Prayer their own act of faith and worship.

Eucharistic Prayer III

Section 1: Summary and Explanation

Eucharistic Prayer III was composed after the Second Vatican Council and introduced in the 1970 Missal of Pope Paul VI. Unlike Eucharistic Prayer II, which is very concise, this prayer is longer, more solemn, and rich in imagery. It quickly became one of the most frequently used Eucharistic Prayers at Sunday Mass because of its balance of reverence, flexibility, and clarity.

Its style reflects the Roman tradition but also draws on Eastern liturgical influences. It places strong emphasis on the sanctifying power of the Holy Spirit, the unity of the Church, and the offering of Christ's sacrifice for the salvation of the world.

Theological Themes

1. **Holiness of God** — God is praised as the source of all holiness.

2. **Sanctification by the Holy Spirit** — the Spirit is invoked to transform the bread and wine.

3. **Sacrifice of Christ** — the Eucharist is described as a holy and living sacrifice.

4. **Unity of the Church** — prayers for the Pope, bishop, clergy, and all the faithful are central.

5. **Prayer for the Dead** — remembrance of those who have died in Christ.

6. **Glory of the Trinity** — concludes with the doxology, giving honor to the Father, Son, and Spirit.

Structure Overview

1. Preface dialogue and Sanctus.

2. Epiclesis (calling down the Spirit on the gifts).

3. Institution Narrative (consecration of bread and wine).

4. Anamnesis and Oblation (memorial of Christ's death and resurrection, offering the sacrifice).

5. Intercessions (Church, living, dead, saints).

6. Doxology (final Trinitarian praise with the Great Amen).

Gestures and Postures

● The priest extends his hands over the gifts at the epiclesis.

● Host and Chalice are elevated at consecration for adoration.

● The faithful kneel during the consecration.

● The priest raises Host and Chalice at the doxology, with the people responding Amen.

Section 2: Full Latin Text with Rubrics and Commentary

Preface Dialogue and Sanctus

Sacerdos:

Dominus vobiscum.

Populus:

Et cum spiritu tuo.

Sacerdos:

Sursum corda.

Populus:

Habemus ad Dominum.

Sacerdos:

Gratias agamus Domino Deo nostro.

Populus:

Dignum et iustum est.

(Then follows the Preface of the day, ending with the Sanctus.)

Omnes:

Sanctus, Sanctus, Sanctus Dominus Deus Sabaoth.

Pleni sunt caeli et terra gloria tua.

Hosanna in excelsis.

Benedictus qui venit in nomine Domini.

Hosanna in excelsis.

Epiclesis

Sacerdos, extensis manibus super oblata:

Vere Sanctus es, Domine, et merito te laudat omnis a te condita creatura,

quia per Filium tuum Dominum nostrum Iesum Christum,

Spiritus Sancti operante virtute, vivificas et sanctificas universa,

et populum tibi congregare non desinis,

ut a solis ortu usque ad occasum oblatio munda offeratur nomini tuo.

(He joins his hands, extends them over the bread and wine, and continues.)

Supplices ergo te, Domine, deprecamur,

ut haec munera, quae tibi sacranda detulimus,

eodem Spiritus Sancti rore sanctificare digneris,

ut Corpus et + Sanguis fiant Filii tui Domini nostri Iesu Christi,

cuius mandato haec mysteria celebramus.

Institution Narrative

Ipse enim, in qua nocte tradebatur,

accepit panem,

et tibi gratias agens benedixit, fregit,

deditque discipulis suis, dicens:

Accipite et manducate ex hoc omnes:

hoc est enim Corpus meum,

quod pro vobis tradetur.

(The priest elevates the Host for adoration, places it on the paten, and genuflects.)

Simili modo, postquam cenatum est,

accipiens calicem,

et tibi gratias agens benedixit,

dedit discipulis suis, dicens:

Accipite et bibite ex eo omnes:

hic est enim calix Sanguinis mei,

novi et aeterni testamenti,

qui pro vobis et pro multis effundetur

in remissionem peccatorum.

Hoc facite in meam commemorationem.

(The priest elevates the chalice for adoration, places it on the corporal, and genuflects.)

Anamnesis and Oblation

Sacerdos:

Memores igitur, Domine, eiusdem Filii tui salutiferae passionis

necnon mirabilis resurrectionis et ascensionis in caelum,

sed et praestolantes alterum eius adventum,

offerimus tibi, gratias referentes,

hoc sacrificium vivum et sanctum.

Respice, quaesumus, in oblationem Ecclesiae tuae,

et agnoscens Hostiam, cuius voluisti immolatione placari,

concede ut, qui Corpore et Sanguine Filii tui reficimur,

Spiritu eius Sancto repleti, unum corpus et unus spiritus inveniamur in Christo.

Intercessions

Ipse nos tibi perficiat munus aeternum,

ut cum electis tuis hereditatem consequi valeamus,

in primis cum beatissima Virgine, Dei Genetrice, Maria,

cum beatis Apostolis tuis et gloriosis Martyribus,

(cum Sancto N.) et omnibus Sanctis,

quorum intercessione perpetuo apud te confidimus adiuvari.

Haec Hostia nostrae reconciliationis proficiat, quaesumus, Domine,

ad totius mundi pacem atque salutem.

Ecclesiam tuam peregrinantem in terra in fide et caritate firmare digneris,

cum Papa nostro N. et Episcopo nostro N.,

cum episcopali ordine et universo clero

et omni populo acquisitionis tuae.

Votis huius familiae, quam tibi astare voluisti, adesto propitius.

Omnes filios tuos ubique dispersos tibi, clemens Pater, miseratus coniunge.

Memento fratrum nostrorum,

qui in spe resurrectionis dormierunt,

omniumque defunctorum,

quorum fidem tu solus cognovisti;

eos in lumen vultus tui admitte et in resurrectione dona eis plenitudinem vitae.

Nobis quoque, peccatoribus famulis tuis,

spem beatam largire,

ut, cum Christi tuis electis consociare digneris,

et gloria tua perfrui sine fine concedas.

Doxology

Sacerdos, elevans patenam cum Hostia et calicem:

Per ipsum, et cum ipso, et in ipso,

est tibi Deo Patri omnipotenti,

in unitate Spiritus Sancti,

omnis honor et gloria,

per omnia saecula saeculorum.

Populus:

Amen.

Explanatory Commentary (English)

- **Epiclesis:** God is praised as the source of all holiness. The Spirit is called down upon the gifts to make them the Body and Blood of Christ.

- **Institution Narrative:** The priest recounts the Last Supper with Christ's words of consecration. At this moment, transubstantiation occurs. Host and chalice are elevated for adoration.

- **Anamnesis and Oblation:** The Church remembers Christ's Passion, Resurrection, and Ascension, and looks forward to His coming again. The Eucharist is offered as a living and holy sacrifice, uniting the faithful into one body in Christ through the Spirit.

- **Intercessions:** Prayers are made for the Church, the Pope, bishops, clergy, and all the faithful. The saints are invoked, reminding the Church of her communion with heaven. Prayers are also offered for the dead, asking that they may share eternal life.

- **Doxology:** The prayer concludes with the raising of the Eucharist and a hymn of glory to the Father through Christ in the Spirit. The congregation's "Amen" seals the entire prayer, uniting priest and people in one act of worship.

Eucharistic Prayer IV

Section 1: Summary and Explanation

Eucharistic Prayer IV was introduced in the Roman Missal of 1970, after the Second Vatican Council. It is unique among the four main prayers because of its sweeping presentation of salvation history, from creation to redemption in Christ, and its emphasis on God's universal plan of salvation. Its structure is modeled on some of the Eastern anaphoras (Eucharistic prayers), particularly that of St. Basil.

This prayer has a fixed Preface, unlike the others, and therefore cannot be combined with seasonal prefaces. It is usually chosen for Sundays in Ordinary Time when the celebrant wishes to highlight God's saving plan and the unity of creation and redemption.

Theological Themes

1. **Creation and Providence** — God is acknowledged as the Creator of all things, who

never ceases to care for His creatures.

2. **Salvation History** — the prayer recounts God's covenant with humanity, the prophets, and the coming of Christ.

3. **Christ's Mission** — Jesus is proclaimed as Savior who preached, healed, and established the New Covenant.

4. **The Holy Spirit** — invoked to sanctify the gifts and unite the faithful in communion.

5. **Universal Salvation** — strong emphasis on God's will that all people be saved and come to the knowledge of the truth.

6. **Communion of Saints** — the faithful on earth, those who have died, and the saints in glory are all remembered in prayer.

Structure Overview

1. Preface (fixed, cannot be replaced).

2. Sanctus.

3. Epiclesis (invocation of the Spirit on the gifts).

4. Institution Narrative and Consecration.

5. Anamnesis (memorial of Christ's Passion, Resurrection, and Ascension).

6. Offering and Intercessions (for Church, living, dead, saints).

7. Doxology with the Great Amen.

Gestures and Postures

- The priest extends hands over the offerings during the epiclesis.

- Bread and chalice are elevated at consecration, with priest and people kneeling in adoration.

- The Eucharist is raised again at the doxology, as the people acclaim the Great Amen.

Section 2: Full Latin Text with Rubrics and Commentary

Preface (fixed) and Sanctus

Sacerdos:

Dominus vobiscum.

Populus:

Et cum spiritu tuo.

Sacerdos:

Sursum corda.

Populus:

Habemus ad Dominum.

Sacerdos:

Gratias agamus Domino Deo nostro.

Populus:

Dignum et iustum est.

Sacerdos:

Vere dignum est tibi gratias agere,

vere iustum est te glorificare, Pater sancte,

quia unus es Deus vivus et verus,

qui es ante saecula et permanes in aeternum,

habitans lucem inaccessibilem.

Tu, qui unus bonus et fons vitae,

omnia fecisti, ut creaturas tuas benedictionibus adimpleres

multasque laetificares tuae claritatis visione.

Et ideo in conspectu tuo innumerabiles assistunt Angeli,

qui die ac nocte tibi serviunt,

et, vultus tui gloriam contemplantes,

te incessanter glorificant.

Cum quibus et nos, et in voce confessionis,

et in exsultatione coniuncti,

omnes exercitus spirituales celebramus, clamantes:

Omnes:

Sanctus, Sanctus, Sanctus Dominus Deus Sabaoth.

Pleni sunt caeli et terra gloria tua.

Hosanna in excelsis.

Benedictus qui venit in nomine Domini.

Hosanna in excelsis.

Epiclesis

Sacerdos, extensis manibus super oblata:

Confitemur tibi, Pater sancte, quia magnus es,

et omnia opera tua sapientia et caritate fecisti.

Hominem ad tuam imaginem condidisti,

et ei commisisti mundi curam universi,

ut, tibi soli Creatori serviret,

et creaturis omnibus imperaret.

Et cum, inobedientia a te deficiens, amisisset amicitias tuae,

non eum dereliquisti in mortis imperio.

Omnibus enim misericorditer subvenisti,

ut te quaerentem inveniret.

Multoties hominibus foedus obtulisti,

et per Prophetas docuisti,

adventum exspectari salutis.

Et sic, Pater sancte, mundum tantopere dilexisti,

ut, plenitudo temporis advenerat,

Filium tuum unigenitum mitteres nobis Salvatorem.

(He extends hands over the bread and wine.)

Rogamus ergo te, Domine,

ut haec munera Spiritus tui sanctificatione consecrentur,

ut Corpus et + Sanguis fiant

Domini nostri Iesu Christi,

ad magnum hoc mysterium celebrandum,

quod ipse nobis reliquit

in foedere novo sempiternaque.

Institution Narrative

Ipse enim, in qua nocte tradebatur,

accepit panem,

tibi gratias egit, benedixit, fregit,

deditque discipulis suis, dicens:

Accipite et manducate ex hoc omnes:

hoc est enim Corpus meum,

quod pro vobis tradetur.

(Elevates Host for adoration, places it on paten, genuflects.)

Simili modo, postquam cenatum est,

accipiens calicem,

tibi gratias egit, benedixit,

dedit discipulis suis, dicens:

Accipite et bibite ex eo omnes:

hic est enim calix Sanguinis mei,

novi et aeterni testamenti,

qui pro vobis et pro multis effundetur

in remissionem peccatorum.

Hoc facite in meam commemorationem.

(Elevates chalice for adoration, places it on corporal, genuflects.)

Anamnesis and Offering

Sacerdos:

Memores igitur, Domine,

ipsius Filii tui salutiferae passionis,

necnon mirabilis resurrectionis

et ascensionis in caelum,

sed et, exspectantes alterum eius adventum,

offerimus tibi, gratias referentes,

hoc sacrificium vivum et sanctum.

Respice, Domine, in oblationem Ecclesiae tuae,

et, agnoscens Hostiam,

cuius immolatione voluisti placari,

concede ut, qui Corporis et Sanguinis Filii tui reficimur,

Spiritu eius Sancto repleti,

unum corpus et unus spiritus inveniamur in Christo.

Intercessions

Ipse nos tibi perficiat munus aeternum,

ut cum electis tuis hereditatem consequi valeamus,

in primis cum beatissima Virgine, Dei Genetrice, Maria,

cum Apostolis tuis et Martyribus,

(et cum Sancto N.)

et omnibus Sanctis,

quorum intercessione perpetuo apud te confidimus adiuvari.

Ad hunc igitur sacrificium reconciliationis nostrae,

quaesumus, Domine,

totus mundus pacem et salutem consequatur.

Ecclesiam tuam peregrinantem in terra

in fide et caritate firmare digneris

cum Papa nostro N.

et Episcopo nostro N.,

cum omnibus Episcopis, universoque clero,

et omni populo acquisitionis tuae.

Votis huius familiae,

quam tibi astare voluisti, adesto propitius.

Omnes filios tuos ubique dispersos,

tibi, Pater clementissime, miseratus coniunge.

Memento omnium filiorum tuorum defunctorum,

quorum fidem tu solus cognovisti;

eos in regnum tuum admitte,

ubi fore speramus,

ut simul gloria tua perfruamur in aeternum.

Doxology

Sacerdos, elevans patenam cum Hostia et calicem:

Per ipsum, et cum ipso, et in ipso,

est tibi Deo Patri omnipotenti,

in unitate Spiritus Sancti,

omnis honor et gloria,

per omnia saecula saeculorum.

Populus:

Amen.

Explanatory Commentary (English)

- **Preface:** This lengthy introduction praises God as Creator and recounts His saving plan through history. It prepares the faithful to hear the central mystery of Christ's sacrifice.

- **Epiclesis:** The Spirit is invoked to sanctify the bread and wine. The priest's extended hands show the descent of the Spirit upon the gifts.

- **Institution Narrative:** Christ's words at the Last Supper are proclaimed. The faithful kneel in adoration as the bread and wine become the Body and Blood of Christ.

- **Anamnesis and Offering:** The Church recalls Christ's Passion, Resurrection, and Ascension and offers His sacrifice anew, asking to be made one body in the Spirit.

- **Intercessions:** The prayer broadens to include the entire Church — living and dead, saints in heaven, and the faithful on earth. It emphasizes peace, unity, and salvation for the whole world.

- **Doxology:** The Eucharistic Prayer culminates in Trinitarian praise, with the people sealing the prayer by their Great Amen.

Chapter 7 – Concluding Rites

The Concluding Rites bring the celebration of the Mass to its formal end. While brief, they carry deep meaning, reminding the faithful that the Eucharist is not only to be celebrated but also lived out in daily life. Having been nourished by Christ in Word and Sacrament, the people are now sent forth to bring His presence into the world. The rites typically include announcements, the priest's blessing, and the dismissal. Each element reinforces the truth that the Mass is both a sacred encounter with God and a commissioning to mission in the everyday circumstances of life.

Announcements

Before the final blessing, it is customary for the priest, deacon, or another minister to make necessary announcements. These are not part of the liturgical prayer itself but serve a pastoral function, keeping the community informed and united. Because the Eucharist is the "source and summit" of the Christian life, parish life naturally flows from it. Thus, announcements are given in this context, linking the worship of God with the ongoing life and mission of the Church.

Announcements may include reminders about upcoming feast days, parish activities, opportunities for service, or catechetical programs. They can also highlight needs of the community, such as requests for volunteers, support for the poor, or special devotions during a liturgical season. Care should be taken that announcements are kept brief, clear, and relevant, so as not to detract from the solemnity of the liturgy.

Even though they are practical in nature, announcements play an important role. They help ensure that the faith celebrated at the altar extends into concrete action throughout the week. They also foster a sense of belonging by keeping the faithful connected to the wider parish family. In this way, the announcements act as a bridge between the sacred celebration and the lived mission of discipleship in the world.

Final Blessing (Full Texts and Variations)

The Final Blessing is one of the most important elements of the Concluding Rites. Having received the Word of God and the Eucharist, the faithful are now sent forth with the blessing of the Lord to live out what they have celebrated. The priest extends his hands over the congregation, invoking God's protection, peace, and grace. The blessing is not simply a polite farewell but a real imparting of divine favor, preparing the people to return to daily life strengthened by the liturgy.

The **simple blessing** is the form used most often:

Priest: *Dominus vobiscum.*

People: *Et cum spiritu tuo.*

Priest: *Benedicat vos omnipotens Deus, Pater, et Filius,* ✠ *et Spiritus Sanctus.*

People: *Amen.*

Here, the priest makes the Sign of the Cross over the people as he pronounces the blessing.

On certain occasions, the Church provides **solemn blessings** or **prayers over the people**. These may involve multiple invocations, with the congregation responding "Amen" after each. For example, during Advent, a solemn blessing might emphasize joyful expectation of Christ's coming. During Lent, the blessing may highlight repentance and

God's mercy. At Easter, the blessing may focus on the joy of the Resurrection and the gift of new life.

An example of a **solemn blessing for Easter Time**:

Priest: *May Almighty God bless you through today's Easter Solemnity and, in His compassion, defend you from every assault of sin.*

People: *Amen.*

Priest: *And may He, who restores you to eternal life in the Resurrection of His Only Begotten, endow you with the prize of immortality.*

People: *Amen.*

Priest: *Now that the days of the Lord's Passion have drawn to a close, may you, who celebrate the gladness of the Paschal Feast, come with Christ's help, and exult in spirit to those feasts that are celebrated in eternal joy.*

People: *Amen.*

Priest: *And may the blessing of Almighty God, the Father, and the Son, ✠ and the Holy Spirit, come down on you and remain with you forever.*

People: *Amen.*

There are also **special blessings** for occasions such as weddings, ordinations, baptisms, confirmations, and funerals. These connect the sacrament just received or celebrated with the ongoing life of the faithful.

The variations of the Final Blessing show the richness of the Church's prayer. Whether simple or solemn, the blessing is always a moment of sending — a reminder that the faithful carry the presence of Christ into the world. The words, the gesture of the extended hands, and the Sign of the Cross all emphasize that God's protection and grace accompany His people as they depart from the liturgy to continue their mission of discipleship.

Dismissal Formulas

The dismissal is the final act of the Mass. It is not a casual ending, but a true commissioning. The Latin word *missa*, from which we get "Mass," comes from this very moment: *Ite, missa est* — "Go, it is sent." The Church understands the dismissal as a call to mission. Having encountered Christ in Word and Sacrament, the faithful are now sent to live the Gospel in the world.

The priest (or deacon if present) proclaims one of the approved formulas. The most common are:

- *Ite, missa est.* – "Go forth, the Mass is ended."

- *Ite in pace, glorificando vita vestra Dominum.* – "Go in peace, glorifying the Lord by your life."

- *Ite ad Evangelium Domini nuntiandum.* – "Go and announce the Gospel of the Lord."

- *Ite in pace.* – "Go in peace."

Each formula has its own emphasis: the first simply marks the conclusion of the liturgy, the second highlights living the faith in daily life, the third stresses evangelization, and the fourth expresses the peace of Christ carried into the world.

The people respond with a strong "Thanks be to God," (*Deo gratias*). This response is more than polite gratitude; it is a joyful acknowledgment of what God has done in the Mass and a readiness to accept the mission that follows.

The dismissal is often accompanied by a **recessional hymn** as the priest and ministers process out. This is not required, but it is customary in many places. The hymn reinforces the sense of joy and mission, sending the community forth with hearts uplifted.

Some parishes conclude with silence after the dismissal, encouraging private thanksgiving. Others continue with music to express joy. Both practices are acceptable as long as the spirit of the dismissal — sending forth for mission — is preserved.

The dismissal reminds us that the Mass does not truly end. It continues in the daily lives of the faithful, in acts of charity, prayer, and witness. The Eucharist celebrated at the altar becomes the Eucharist lived in the world. The words "Go in peace" are not simply a farewell; they are a charge to bring Christ's peace and presence into every corner of life.

Reverent Departure from the Church

After the dismissal, the faithful are invited to leave the church, but this departure is not meant to be hurried or casual. The reverent way in which the people depart reflects their awareness that they have just participated in the most sacred act of Christian worship. The Mass has ended, but its fruits are meant to flow into daily life.

Traditionally, the faithful remain standing until the priest and ministers have left the sanctuary. Many Catholics choose to kneel briefly in silent thanksgiving before leaving their pews, offering a personal prayer of gratitude for the gift of Holy Communion. This moment of quiet reflection helps the graces of the Eucharist take root in the heart before the distractions of ordinary life resume.

As they exit, the faithful customarily **genuflect toward the tabernacle**, where the Blessed Sacrament is reserved. This act of reverence is a visible sign of belief in the Real Presence of Christ. If the tabernacle is not in the main sanctuary, a bow toward the altar is appropriate. These gestures remind the faithful that they remain in God's house until they step outside, and that their conduct should reflect the sacredness of the space.

The manner of leaving the church also carries meaning. Conversations and greetings are best saved for outside the worship space, allowing the church to remain a place of prayer for those who wish to linger. Families are encouraged to leave together, showing that the Eucharist strengthens not only individuals but also the domestic Church.

Hymns or instrumental music may accompany the recessional, adding to the sense of joy and mission. Whether in silence or in song, the departure is marked by dignity and gratitude.

The reverent departure reminds the faithful that the liturgy does not end with the closing hymn or the final blessing. They are sent forth to live the Eucharist in their homes, workplaces, and communities. Every act of love, service, and witness in the week ahead becomes an extension of what was celebrated at the altar. Leaving the church reverently is thus both a gesture of respect for God's presence and an acknowledgment of the mission entrusted to every Catholic: to go in peace and glorify the Lord by their life.

PART 3
Prayers and Devotions

Chapter 8 – All the People's Parts in Order

One of the main goals of this book is to make the Mass accessible so that every Catholic can participate with confidence and devotion. Many who attend Mass, whether newcomers, those returning after time away, or even lifelong Catholics, sometimes feel unsure about exactly what to say, when to respond, or how to join in fully with the community. The responses of the faithful, though often short, are essential. They form a dialogue between the priest and the people, uniting the whole congregation in one voice of prayer.

This chapter gathers **all the people's parts of the Mass in order**, from the very beginning of the Introductory Rites through the final dismissal. By presenting them in a single sequence, you will have an easy reference that shows you what to say at each step and how to respond to the priest or deacon. Alongside the words, this chapter also notes the postures and gestures — standing, sitting, kneeling, bowing, making the Sign of the Cross — so that you can follow with your whole body as well as your voice.

Think of this chapter as a **quick-reference guide** or "cheat sheet" for the Mass. It allows you to see the flow of the liturgy at a glance and helps you grow more familiar with the rhythm of Catholic worship. When the words and gestures become natural, you are freer to pray with the heart, to enter deeply into the mystery being celebrated, and to participate with the reverence and joy the Church invites from all her members.

Quick-Reference List of Every Response in the Mass

This section gathers all of the people's parts in the order in which they appear at Mass. It allows the faithful to follow the entire liturgy without confusion and to participate fully with their voices and gestures. Each response is short, but together they form the prayer of the whole Church.

Introductory Rites

● **Sign of the Cross**

Priest: *In the name of the Father, and of the Son, and of the Holy Spirit.*

People: *Amen.*

● **Greeting**

Priest: *The Lord be with you.*

People: *And with your spirit.*

● **Penitential Act**

People (Confiteor): *I confess to almighty God...*

Priest: *Lord, have mercy.*

People: *Lord, have mercy.*

Priest: *Christ, have mercy.*

People: *Christ, have mercy.*

Priest: *Lord, have mercy.*

People: *Lord, have mercy.*

- **Gloria (when prescribed)**

People: *Glory to God in the highest...* (recited or sung together).

- **Collect**

Priest: *Let us pray.*

People: *Amen.*

Liturgy of the Word

- **First and Second Readings**

Reader: *The Word of the Lord.*

People: *Thanks be to God.*

- **Responsorial Psalm**

Cantor: verse of the psalm.

People: refrain response (e.g., *The Lord is my shepherd; there is nothing I shall want.*).

- **Gospel Acclamation**

People: *Alleluia* (or a seasonal acclamation during Lent).

- **Gospel Reading**

Deacon/Priest: *The Lord be with you.*

People: *And with your spirit.*

Deacon/Priest: *A reading from the holy Gospel according to N.*

People: *Glory to you, O Lord.*

At the end: *The Gospel of the Lord.*

People: *Praise to you, Lord Jesus Christ.*

- **Homily** – no response.

- **Profession of Faith (on Sundays and solemnities)**

People: *I believe in one God...* (Nicene Creed or Apostles' Creed).

- **Prayer of the Faithful**

Reader: *We pray to the Lord.*

People: *Lord, hear our prayer.*

Liturgy of the Eucharist

- Presentation of the Gifts

Priest: *Pray, brothers and sisters, that my sacrifice and yours may be acceptable to God, the almighty Father.*

People: *May the Lord accept the sacrifice at your hands for the praise and glory of his name, for our good and the good of all his holy Church.*

- Preface Dialogue

Priest: *The Lord be with you.*

People: *And with your spirit.*

Priest: *Lift up your hearts.*

People: *We lift them up to the Lord.*

Priest: *Let us give thanks to the Lord our God.*

People: *It is right and just.*

- **Sanctus**

People: *Holy, Holy, Holy Lord God of hosts...*

- **Memorial Acclamation (after consecration)**

Priest: *The mystery of faith.*

People (choose one):

o   *We proclaim your Death, O Lord, and profess your Resurrection until you come again.*

o   *When we eat this Bread and drink this Cup, we proclaim your Death, O Lord, until you come again.*

o   *Save us, Savior of the world, for by your Cross and Resurrection you have set us free.*

- **Doxology and Great Amen**

Priest: *Through him, and with him, and in him...*

People: *Amen.*

Communion Rite

- **Lord's Prayer**

People: *Our Father, who art in heaven...*

- **Embolism Response**

Priest: *Deliver us, Lord, we pray...*

People: *For the kingdom, the power and the glory are yours now and forever.*

- **Sign of Peace**

Priest: *The peace of the Lord be with you always.*

People: *And with your spirit.*

- **Agnus Dei**

People: *Lamb of God, you take away the sins of the world, have mercy on us... grant us peace.*

- **Communion**

Minister: *The Body of Christ.*

People: *Amen.*

Minister: *The Blood of Christ.*

People: *Amen.*

Concluding Rites

- **Blessing**

Priest: *The Lord be with you.*

People: *And with your spirit.*

Priest: *May almighty God bless you, the Father, and the Son, and the Holy Spirit.*

People: *Amen.*

- **Dismissal**

Deacon/Priest: *Go forth, the Mass is ended.* (or another formula).

People: *Thanks be to God.*

This quick-reference list gives every spoken part of the people during the Mass, from the first *Amen* to the final *Thanks be to God*. By learning and praying these responses, the faithful take their active role in the liturgy, fulfilling the call to worship God with one heart and one voice.

When to Stand, Sit, or Kneel (Includes Full Kneeling Instructions)

Catholic worship involves the whole body, not only the voice and mind. Postures such as standing, sitting, and kneeling express outwardly the faith that is professed inwardly. They are not arbitrary but meaningful actions that unite the congregation in a common act of prayer. Knowing when to stand, sit, or kneel helps the faithful participate reverently and confidently in the liturgy.

Standing

Standing is the ancient posture of respect, readiness, and prayer. It is used throughout the Mass to show reverence and attentiveness. The faithful stand:

- At the beginning of Mass, for the **Sign of the Cross** and the **Greeting**.

- During the **Gospel Acclamation** and Gospel reading, honoring Christ who speaks in His Word.

- For the **Creed** on Sundays and solemnities.

- At the **Prayer of the Faithful**.

- During the **Preface Dialogue** and the **Sanctus**.

- From the **Lord's Prayer** until after the Sign of Peace, unless kneeling is customary during the Agnus Dei.

- For the **Concluding Rites** and the **Dismissal**.

Sitting

Sitting is a posture of listening, meditation, and quiet attentiveness. The faithful sit:

- During the readings before the Gospel.

- For the **Responsorial Psalm**, if not sung standing.

- During the **Homily**.

- During the **Preparation of the Gifts** (offertory), until the priest invites all to stand for the Prayer over the Offerings.

- After receiving Holy Communion, for personal thanksgiving (though kneeling in prayer is also acceptable).

Kneeling

Kneeling is the posture of adoration and humility. It expresses reverence before the Real Presence of Christ. The Church in many countries requires the faithful to kneel at certain points, though customs may vary by region. The most common practice is:

- **From after the Sanctus until after the elevation of the Chalice**. In the United States and many other countries, the faithful remain kneeling through the entire Eucharistic Prayer until the Great Amen.

- At the **"Behold the Lamb of God"** before Communion, as an act of adoration before approaching the altar.

- After returning to one's place from receiving Communion, many remain kneeling in silent thanksgiving, though sitting is also permitted.

Full Kneeling Instructions

- Kneel with both knees on the ground, keeping the back upright and hands folded in prayer.

- Avoid slouching, leaning heavily, or resting on the pew in front unless physically necessary.

- Rising and kneeling together with the congregation shows unity and discipline, making the posture a true communal act of worship.

- Those unable to kneel due to age, illness, or disability may sit reverently instead; participation of the heart is what matters most.

Each posture in the Mass has meaning: **standing** shows readiness and reverence, **sitting** fosters attentive listening and reflection, and **kneeling** expresses deep adoration. By observing these postures faithfully, Catholics allow their bodies to join their voices and hearts in worship. This harmony of prayer, gesture, and movement enriches the liturgy and strengthens the unity of the whole assembly gathered around the altar of the Lord.

Chapter 9 – Common Catholic Prayers

Catholic life of prayer extends beyond the liturgy of the Mass into daily devotion. For centuries, the faithful have turned to short, powerful prayers to express their love of God, seek His help, and keep His presence alive throughout the day. These traditional prayers are treasured because they are simple to learn yet profound in meaning. They can be prayed alone or with others, at home or in church, in moments of joy and in times of need.

This chapter gathers the most common Catholic prayers, beginning with those every Catholic child learns — the *Our Father*, the *Hail Mary*, and the *Glory Be*. These prayers form the foundation of Christian devotion. They are recited in the Rosary, in communal prayer, and in countless personal moments of faith. By learning and meditating on them, the faithful enter more deeply into the heart of Catholic spirituality, joining countless generations who have lifted these words to God.

Our Father, Hail Mary, Glory Be

The Our Father

The *Our Father* is the prayer taught by Jesus Himself when His disciples asked Him how to pray (Matthew 6:9–13; Luke 11:2–4). It is called the "perfect prayer" because it contains all the elements of Christian prayer: praise of God, trust in His will, requests for daily needs, forgiveness, and protection from evil.

- **Meaning**: When we say "Our Father," we acknowledge God as Father of all and ourselves as brothers and sisters in Christ. Asking for "daily bread" includes both physical nourishment and the Eucharist. Praying for forgiveness reminds us to forgive others. Asking deliverance from evil affirms God's power over sin and Satan.

- **Use in Catholic life**: It is recited at every Mass, in the Rosary, in morning and evening prayer, and often at the beginning or end of gatherings.

The Hail Mary

The *Hail Mary* is a prayer of devotion to the Blessed Virgin Mary, Mother of God. Its words come from Scripture: the greeting of the angel Gabriel at the Annunciation (Luke 1:28) and the greeting of Elizabeth at the Visitation (Luke 1:42). The Church added the petition for Mary's intercession.

- **Meaning**: The prayer praises Mary for her unique role in salvation history and asks her to intercede for us "now and at the hour of our death." By calling her "full of grace" and "blessed among women," we honor her holiness. Asking her prayers reflects our belief in the communion of saints, that those in heaven pray for those on earth.

- **Use in Catholic life**: Central to the Rosary, often recited at the close of daily prayer, and prayed in times of need for Mary's maternal protection.

The Glory Be

The *Glory Be*, or *Doxology*, is a short prayer praising the Trinity: Father, Son, and Holy Spirit. Its simplicity and rhythm make it easy to memorize, and it is often used to conclude psalms, hymns, or other prayers.

- **Text**: "Glory be to the Father, and to the Son, and to the Holy Spirit, as it was in the beginning, is now, and ever shall be, world without end. Amen."

- **Meaning**: This prayer affirms the eternal nature of God and honors His glory from creation through eternity. It reminds us that all prayer, no matter how long or short, ends in praise of the Trinity.

- **Use in Catholic life**: Recited at the end of psalms and prayers in the Liturgy of the Hours, and included in each decade of the Rosary.

Together, the *Our Father*, *Hail Mary*, and *Glory Be* form the foundation of Catholic devotion. They are the first prayers many Catholics learn and the last prayers whispered at life's end. By repeating them daily, the faithful unite themselves with the prayer of Christ, the intercession of Mary, and the eternal praise of the Trinity.

Prayer to Saint Michael

The *Prayer to Saint Michael the Archangel* is one of the most beloved devotions of the Church. It was composed by Pope Leo XIII in 1886 after a vision that impressed upon him the reality of spiritual warfare. For decades, it was recited at the end of Masses worldwide, and today it is still encouraged as a powerful protection against evil.

The text invokes Saint Michael, the leader of the heavenly hosts, to defend the faithful against the snares of the devil. It acknowledges that Christian life involves real spiritual struggles, but that God provides His angels to guard and protect His people.

- **Text**: "Saint Michael the Archangel, defend us in battle. Be our protection against the wickedness and snares of the devil; may God rebuke him, we humbly pray; and do thou, O Prince of the heavenly host, by the power of God, cast into hell Satan and all the evil spirits who prowl about the world seeking the ruin of souls. Amen."

- **Meaning**: The prayer combines humility (asking for God's rebuke) with confidence in Saint Michael's intercession. It reminds the faithful that evil is real but not stronger than God's power.

- **Use in Catholic life**: Often prayed after Mass, before traveling, or during times of temptation or fear. It serves as a reminder of God's protection and the presence of His angels.

Act of Contrition

The *Act of Contrition* is a prayer expressing sorrow for sins and a firm purpose to amend one's life. It is most commonly prayed during the Sacrament of Reconciliation, after confessing sins and before receiving absolution. However, it is also appropriate for daily prayer, especially before bed, as a way to examine the conscience and ask God's mercy.

The Church provides several approved versions, but they all contain the same essential elements: sorrow for sin, recognition of its offense against God, trust in His mercy, and a resolve to avoid sin and its occasions.

- **Traditional text**: "O my God, I am heartily sorry for having offended Thee, and I detest all my sins because I dread the loss of heaven and the pains of hell, but most of all because they offend Thee, my God, who art all good and deserving of all my love. I firmly resolve, with the help of Thy grace, to confess my sins, to do penance, and to amend my life. Amen."

- **Meaning**: The prayer balances fear of sin's consequences with love for God, who deserves obedience and devotion. It makes clear that true contrition involves both sorrow and a desire to change.

- **Use in Catholic life**: Required in confession, recommended in nightly prayer, and helpful whenever one feels the need to return to God's mercy.

Both the Prayer to Saint Michael and the Act of Contrition are short yet profound prayers, reminding the faithful of two vital truths: that we live in a spiritual battle needing God's protection, and that repentance and conversion open the door to His infinite mercy.

How to Pray the Rosary (Step-by-Step)

The Rosary is one of the most cherished devotions in Catholic life. It combines vocal prayer with meditation on the mysteries of Christ's life, drawing the faithful closer to Jesus through the intercession of His Blessed Mother. Praying the Rosary regularly strengthens faith, brings peace, and helps one to contemplate the Gospel in a deep and personal way.

Step 1: Begin with the Sign of the Cross

Hold the crucifix, make the Sign of the Cross, and pray the **Apostles' Creed**. This affirms the faith upon which the Rosary is built.

Step 2: Pray the Introductory Prayers

On the first large bead, pray the **Our Father**.

On the next three small beads, pray three **Hail Marys**, offering them for faith, hope, and charity.

On the next large bead, pray the **Glory Be**.

Step 3: Announce the First Mystery

Each decade of the Rosary focuses on one mystery from the lives of Jesus and Mary. The mysteries are grouped into four sets:

- **Joyful Mysteries** (Annunciation, Visitation, Nativity, Presentation, Finding in the Temple).

- **Sorrowful Mysteries** (Agony in the Garden, Scourging at the Pillar, Crowning with Thorns, Carrying of the Cross, Crucifixion).

- **Glorious Mysteries** (Resurrection, Ascension, Descent of the Holy Spirit, Assumption, Coronation of Mary).

- **Luminous Mysteries** (Baptism in the Jordan, Wedding at Cana, Proclamation of the Kingdom, Transfiguration, Institution of the Eucharist).

Announce the first mystery for the day's set and pause briefly to meditate.

Step 4: Pray the Decade

On the large bead, pray the **Our Father**.

On each of the next ten small beads, pray a **Hail Mary**, reflecting on the mystery.

After the tenth bead, pray the **Glory Be** and the **Fatima Prayer**: *"O my Jesus, forgive us our sins, save us from the fires of hell, lead all souls to heaven, especially those in most need of thy mercy."*

Step 5: Continue through All Five Mysteries

Repeat the same sequence — announce the mystery, pray the Our Father, ten Hail Marys, the Glory Be, and the Fatima Prayer — for each of the five decades. Each decade takes about five minutes, and the full Rosary about 20–25 minutes.

Step 6: Conclude the Rosary

After completing all five decades, pray the **Hail, Holy Queen**, followed by the concluding prayer: *"O God, whose only begotten Son, by His life, death, and resurrection, has purchased for us the rewards of eternal life; grant, we beseech Thee, that meditating upon these mysteries of the most holy Rosary of the Blessed Virgin Mary, we may imitate* *what they contain and obtain what they promise, through the same Christ our Lord. Amen."*

Finally, make the Sign of the Cross. Some also add the Litany of Loreto or other Marian prayers.

Tips for Praying the Rosary Well

- Pray slowly and reflectively, letting the repetition quiet the mind.

- Meditate on each mystery by imagining the scene, considering what it reveals about Jesus, and asking how it applies to your own life.

- Use Scripture verses, artwork, or meditative reflections to deepen the prayer.

- The Rosary can be prayed alone or in groups, at home, in church, or while traveling.

The Rosary is not simply the repetition of prayers but a meditative journey through the Gospel. By praying it faithfully, Catholics unite themselves to Christ and Mary, grow in virtue, and draw closer to the heart of God.

Chapter 10 – Special Masses and Occasions

While the structure of the Mass remains constant, the Church provides variations for certain occasions that mark important milestones in the life of the faithful. These special celebrations enrich the liturgy with prayers, readings, and rituals that highlight the unique graces of the moment. They remind us that the Eucharist is not isolated from the events of human life but is at the center of them, sanctifying key moments of joy, sorrow, and growth in faith.

Some of the most significant of these occasions include **weddings**, where two people are united in a sacramental covenant; **funerals**, where the Church commends the soul of the departed to God and consoles the living; and **holy days of obligation**, when the Church gathers to celebrate great mysteries of salvation beyond the regular rhythm of Sundays. Additionally, the sacraments of **First Communion** and **Confirmation** are often celebrated within Mass, deepening the connection between the Eucharist and Christian initiation.

By understanding the structure and meaning of these special celebrations, Catholics can participate more fully and appreciate the richness of the liturgy. These occasions show how the Mass adapts to accompany the faithful through every stage of life, from birth to eternal rest in God.

Weddings, Funerals, and Holy Days

The Mass takes on a distinctive character when celebrated for particular life events or solemn observances. While the essential structure of the liturgy never changes, the prayers, readings, and rituals highlight the grace of the occasion.

Weddings

When a wedding is celebrated within Mass, it is known as the **Rite of Marriage with**

Mass. The couple, already baptized, exchange vows in the presence of the Church, and their union is elevated by the reception of the Eucharist. The couple themselves are the ministers of the sacrament, while the priest or deacon acts as a witness.

The nuptial Mass includes special readings chosen to reflect the dignity of Christian marriage, prayers for the spouses, and a solemn blessing over the couple. Often, both bride and groom present gifts to the altar and receive Holy Communion under both kinds. This expresses the profound unity between their married life and Christ's love for His Church, which is celebrated in the Eucharist.

Funerals

The **Funeral Mass**, or *Requiem Mass*, is the central liturgical expression of the Church's prayer for the faithful departed. It entrusts the soul of the deceased to God's mercy, commends them to eternal life, and consoles the living with the hope of the Resurrection.

The liturgy is marked by texts that speak of eternal rest and God's compassion: the entrance chant "Eternal rest grant unto them, O Lord," the prayers of commendation, and the final farewell. The readings emphasize faith in Christ's victory over death. During the procession at the end, the body is honored with incense and holy water, reminders of baptism and the promise of new life.

For Catholic families, the Funeral Mass is not only a time of mourning but also a powerful act of faith, proclaiming that those who die in Christ will live with Him forever.

Holy Days of Obligation

Holy days are feasts of the Lord, the Blessed Virgin Mary, or the saints that the Church commands the faithful to observe with Mass attendance. They include celebrations such as Christmas, the Immaculate Conception, All Saints' Day, and the Assumption of Mary.

On these days, the liturgy takes on a festive character. The Gloria and Creed are recited, special readings appropriate to the feast are proclaimed, and prayers highlight the mystery being celebrated. The faithful are reminded that the rhythm of their worship is not limited to Sundays but includes the great mysteries of salvation throughout the year.

Holy days draw the faithful into the life of the Church universal, uniting them in prayer and worship with Catholics around the world. They also help to sanctify time itself, weaving the story of salvation into the calendar of daily life.

In each of these special Masses — weddings, funerals, and holy days — the Church adapts her liturgy to the needs of her people, while keeping the Eucharist at the center. These occasions show that the Mass is both timeless and responsive, a celebration that accompanies the faithful at every stage of life and every season of the year.

First Communion and Confirmation

The sacraments of **First Holy Communion** and **Confirmation** are milestones in a Catholic's journey of faith. Both are often celebrated within the context of the Mass, highlighting their intimate connection to the Eucharist and to the life of the Church.

First Holy Communion

First Communion is the moment when a baptized Catholic receives the Eucharist for the first time. It is a profound event because the Eucharist is the Body and Blood of Christ, the very heart of Catholic worship and the source of spiritual life. Children are usually prepared through catechesis, learning about the Real Presence of Christ in the Eucharist, the meaning of the Mass, and the importance of approaching Communion with reverence and a clean heart.

The First Communion Mass follows the normal structure of the liturgy but includes special elements. The readings may be chosen to reflect the Eucharist as the Bread of Life, such as John 6. The homily is directed toward the children, explaining in simple but meaningful words what they are about to receive.

The children often take part in the entrance procession, present the gifts of bread and wine, or read the petitions in the Prayer of the Faithful. At Communion, they come forward reverently, usually dressed in white garments symbolizing purity. They receive either on the tongue or in the hand, responding with a clear "Amen" to affirm their faith in the Real Presence.

The celebration continues with prayers of thanksgiving, and in many parishes the newly-communicated children gather afterward for a blessing or photograph. The emphasis is not only on a personal milestone but on becoming fully part of the Eucharistic community of the Church.

Confirmation

The Sacrament of Confirmation strengthens the grace of Baptism and bestows the gifts of the Holy Spirit in fullness. It is often celebrated within Mass, since the Eucharist is the summit of Christian initiation. In Confirmation, the baptized are sealed with the gift of the Spirit and sent forth as mature witnesses of Christ.

During the Confirmation Mass, the candidates are presented after the Gospel and homily. The bishop, or a priest delegated by him, leads the rite. After a renewal of baptismal promises, he extends his hands over the candidates, praying for the outpouring of the Holy Spirit. Then, one by one, the candidates come forward to be anointed with sacred chrism on the forehead. The bishop says, "Be sealed with the Gift of the Holy Spirit," to which the confirmand replies, "Amen." He then greets them with the sign of peace.

Special readings are often chosen, such as from Acts of the Apostles, emphasizing the coming of the Spirit at Pentecost. The entire assembly prays for the candidates, recognizing that Confirmation is not just a personal event but a strengthening of the whole Church.

After the anointing, the Mass continues with the Liturgy of the Eucharist. The newly confirmed, now fully initiated, take part with a deeper sense of belonging and responsibility. They are called to witness to Christ in word and deed, equipped with the Spirit's gifts of wisdom, understanding, counsel, fortitude, knowledge, piety, and fear of the Lord.

First Communion and Confirmation highlight the beauty of Christian initiation. In First Communion, the faithful receive Christ sacramentally for the first time; in Confirmation, they are strengthened by the Spirit to live as active disciples. Both celebrated within Mass show that every step of Catholic life is centered on the Eucharist, drawing the faithful closer to Christ and sending them forth to live as His witnesses.

PART 4
More Prayers and Devotions

Chapter 11 – Reverence and Piety

Reverence and piety are at the heart of fruitful participation in the Mass. They are not simply outward displays of respect but attitudes of the heart that shape the way we encounter God in worship. To be reverent is to recognize the holiness of the mystery before us; to be pious is to let love and devotion flow from that recognition into our words, actions, and way of life.

The Church invites the faithful to approach the liturgy with both inward preparation and outward expression. This includes cultivating a prayerful spirit before arriving at church, examining one's conscience, and being mindful of how we present ourselves physically through posture, gestures, and attire. Every detail, from the silence kept before Mass to the Sign of the Cross made with care, reflects our awareness that we stand in the presence of God.

Reverence and piety draw us closer to Christ and strengthen the witness of the Church.

Preparing for Mass Spiritually and Physically

Participation in the Mass does not begin the moment one enters the church. To fully receive the graces of the Eucharist, the faithful are called to prepare both spiritually and physically. This preparation shapes the heart, mind, and body to enter into the sacred mysteries with reverence and devotion.

Spiritual Preparation

The most important way to prepare for Mass is to approach with a heart open to God. This begins with **prayer before Mass**, which may include reading the day's Scripture readings, praying the Rosary, or offering intentions for the liturgy. Reflecting on what one hopes to bring to the altar — gratitude, struggles, petitions for others — helps the faithful participate consciously and intentionally.

Another essential element is **confession of sins**. The Church encourages frequent reception of the Sacrament of Reconciliation, especially when conscious of grave sin, since one must be in a state of grace to receive Communion worthily. Examining one's conscience before Mass allows the Penitential Act at the beginning of the liturgy to be more sincere.

Spiritual preparation also involves cultivating **silence and recollection**. Arriving early to kneel and pray quietly helps to leave behind distractions. Silence before Mass is not emptiness but space for God's voice. It allows the faithful to enter the liturgy already attentive to His presence.

Physical Preparation

The Church also teaches that preparation involves the body. Catholics are asked to observe the **Eucharistic fast**, refraining from food and drink (except water and medicine) for at least one hour before receiving Communion. This small sacrifice awakens hunger for the Bread of Life and honors the sacredness of the Eucharist.

Rest and attentiveness are also important. Coming to Mass rested and alert shows respect for God and for the community. Parents can help children prepare by explaining what will happen, encouraging reverence, and teaching simple prayers.

Physical presence should reflect inner devotion. Arriving on time, or even early, shows eagerness for the Lord's banquet. Being late or careless with punctuality diminishes the sense of Mass as the highest priority of the week.

Disposition of Heart and Body

Finally, preparation means uniting inward disposition with outward readiness. The faithful bring not only their needs but also their joys, sufferings, and daily labors. As bread and wine represent the work of human hands, so too the faithful place their lives upon the altar.

A well-prepared Catholic comes to Mass spiritually reconciled, prayerful, and recollected, while also physically attentive, rested, and ready. This union of body and soul ensures that worship is not routine but a true encounter with Christ. In this way, preparation transforms the Mass from a weekly obligation into a living encounter with the Lord who calls His people to worship in spirit and truth.

Posture, Gesture, and Attire

The way Catholics carry themselves at Mass — in posture, gesture, and dress — reflects the reverence due to the presence of God. These outward expressions are not superficial; they are signs of inner devotion and help the faithful enter more deeply into the mystery of the Eucharist. By worshiping with the whole body, the faithful unite mind, heart, and spirit in one act of praise.

Posture

Standing expresses readiness, respect, and active participation. Catholics stand for the beginning of Mass, the Gospel, the Profession of Faith, the Prayer of the Faithful, and parts of the Eucharistic Prayer. Standing together as a community symbolizes unity and attentiveness to God's Word.

Sitting is the posture of listening and reflection. The faithful sit during the readings before the Gospel, the homily, and the offertory. It is not a time of rest but of attentiveness, receiving God's Word with open hearts.

Kneeling is the posture of adoration and humility. Catholics kneel during the consecration, and in many places throughout the entire Eucharistic Prayer, as well as before receiving Communion. Kneeling acknowledges Christ's Real Presence in the Eucharist and expresses a heart bowed before the King of kings.

Gestures

The Sign of the Cross begins and ends the Mass, marking the faithful with the name of the Trinity. Making this sign slowly and deliberately is an act of faith, not a casual motion.

Bowing is a sign of reverence. Catholics bow their heads at the name of Jesus and Mary, and make a profound bow before the altar or during the Creed at the words of the Incarnation. Bowing shows humility before God and honor to His holy name.

Genuflection is a gesture reserved for the presence of Christ in the Eucharist. Entering or leaving a pew, the faithful genuflect toward the tabernacle. On Good Friday, genuflection is also made before the cross. This act acknowledges Christ's true presence and expresses worship with the whole body.

The Sign of Peace is another important gesture. With a handshake, bow, or other culturally suitable expression, the faithful show reconciliation and unity before receiving Communion.

The Elevation of the Host and Chalice is accompanied by the gaze of the faithful in adoration. Many silently pray, "My Lord and my God," affirming belief in the Real Presence.

These gestures, repeated week after week, form a rhythm of worship that draws the faithful into the sacred mysteries.

Attire

The way one dresses for Mass also reflects reverence. Attire should be modest, clean, and dignified, showing respect for God and for the sacred assembly. The goal is not formality for its own sake but a visible expression that this is a holy encounter.

- **For men**: long pants and a collared shirt are appropriate; in some cultures, a suit or traditional dress may be worn for solemnity.

- **For women**: modest dresses, skirts, or slacks with blouses are fitting; care should be taken that clothing is neither overly casual nor distracting.

- **For children**: neat, respectful clothing helps instill the sense that Mass is special.

Special occasions such as weddings, funerals, confirmations, and holy days often call for more formal attire, highlighting the significance of the celebration. While cultural norms differ, the guiding principle is always modesty and respect.

Conclusion

Posture, gesture, and attire all contribute to the atmosphere of reverence at Mass. Standing, sitting, and kneeling unite the body with prayer. Gestures such as the Sign of the Cross, bows, and genuflections are physical acts of devotion. Attire reflects the dignity of the liturgy and the awareness that we come before God Himself.

By embracing these outward signs with sincerity, Catholics create a spirit of prayerful unity, where the whole assembly worships with body and soul. Such reverence not only honors the sacred mysteries but also prepares hearts to receive Christ with humility and love.

Chapter 12 – Theology of the Eucharist

The Eucharist is the heart of Catholic life and worship. It is more than a symbol or a ritual; it is the sacrament in which Jesus Christ becomes truly present — Body, Blood, Soul, and Divinity — under the appearances of bread and wine. Through the Eucharist, the faithful are united to Christ's sacrifice on the Cross and nourished with the very life of God. Because of its central place in the Church's life, the Eucharist has been studied, explained, and celebrated with profound devotion throughout the centuries.

To understand the Eucharist deeply, Catholics look first to **Sacred Scripture**, where the roots of the sacrament are found in the Old Testament foreshadowings, the Last Supper narratives, and the teachings of Jesus, especially in John 6. Alongside the Bible, the **Catechism of the Catholic Church** provides a clear and authoritative summary of what the Church believes and teaches about this mystery, drawing from Tradition, the Fathers, and centuries of theological reflection.

In this chapter, we will explore both the biblical foundations and the Catechism's teaching on the Eucharist. Together, they reveal why the Eucharist is called the "source and summit of the Christian life" and how it draws the Church ever closer to Christ.

Biblical Foundations

The Eucharist is not an invention of the Church but a sacrament rooted in the words and actions of Christ and foreshadowed throughout Scripture. From the Old Testament to the New, God prepared His people for the mystery of the Eucharist, and in Jesus the promise was fulfilled. To understand the theology of the Eucharist, we must see how the Bible reveals it as the true sacrifice, the heavenly banquet, and the abiding presence of Christ.

Old Testament Foreshadowings

1.   Melchizedek's Offering

In Genesis 14:18–20, Melchizedek, the king of Salem and a priest of God Most High, brings out bread and wine and blesses Abram. This mysterious priest-king prefigures Christ, the eternal High Priest, who would later offer His Body and Blood under the forms of bread and wine. The Church Fathers saw Melchizedek as a type of Christ and his offering as a shadow of the Eucharist.

2.   The Passover Lamb

In Exodus 12, the Israelites are commanded to sacrifice a lamb and eat it with unleavened bread, marking their doorposts with its blood for deliverance from death. This event prefigures Jesus, the true Lamb of God, whose sacrifice saves us from eternal death. The Eucharist makes present that saving sacrifice, and in receiving the Body and Blood of Christ, the faithful share in the new Passover.

3.   The Manna in the Desert

When Israel wandered in the wilderness, God fed them with manna from heaven (Exodus 16). This bread sustained them physically, but it was temporary. Jesus later identifies Himself as the true Bread from heaven who gives eternal life (John 6:32–35). The manna thus points directly to the Eucharist, which satisfies the deepest hunger of the human soul.

The Teaching of Jesus

1. The Bread of Life Discourse

In John 6, after the miracle of feeding the five thousand, Jesus teaches that He is the Bread of Life. He declares, "Whoever eats my flesh and drinks my blood has eternal life, and I will raise him on the last day" (John 6:54). His listeners struggle with the literal meaning of His words, yet Jesus does not soften His teaching. Instead, He emphasizes its reality: "My flesh is true food, and my blood is true drink" (John 6:55). This discourse prepares the disciples to understand the gift He will give at the Last Supper.

2. The Last Supper

At the heart of the Eucharist is the institution narrative found in the Synoptic Gospels (Matthew 26:26–29; Mark 14:22–25; Luke 22:14–20) and echoed by St. Paul (1 Corinthians 11:23–26). Jesus takes bread and wine, blesses them, and declares them to be His Body and Blood: "This is my Body, which will be given for you… This cup is the new covenant in my Blood." He commands His disciples, "Do this in memory of me." Here Christ establishes the sacrament that would perpetuate His sacrifice and presence in the Church until the end of time.

3. Emmaus and the Breaking of the Bread

After the Resurrection, Jesus appears to two disciples on the road to Emmaus (Luke 24:13–35). They recognize Him not in His teaching but in the breaking of the bread. This encounter demonstrates that the risen Christ is present to His Church in the Eucharist. From the earliest days, the "breaking of bread" became the term used for the Eucharistic celebration (Acts 2:42).

The Apostolic Witness

The first Christians, as recorded in Acts 2:42, "devoted themselves to the apostles' teaching and fellowship, to the breaking of bread and the prayers." The Eucharist was central to their life of faith. St. Paul provides the earliest written account of the institution of the Eucharist in 1 Corinthians 11:23–26. He affirms that the Eucharist proclaims the Lord's death until He comes and warns the faithful to discern the Body of Christ lest they eat and drink judgment upon themselves (1 Corinthians 11:27–29). This teaching confirms the Church's belief in the Real Presence and the necessity of reverent participation.

Sacrifice and Covenant Fulfilled

The Old Covenant sacrifices, from the lamb of Passover to the offerings of the Temple, all point to Christ's perfect sacrifice on the Cross. The Eucharist is the sacramental making-present of that sacrifice. Hebrews 9–10 teaches that Christ entered once for all into the heavenly sanctuary, offering His Blood for eternal redemption. The Mass unites us to that one eternal offering.

By instituting the Eucharist, Christ established the **New Covenant**. As the blood of animals sealed the Old Covenant at Sinai (Exodus 24:8), so the Blood of Christ seals the New Covenant in the Eucharist. Every Mass is a renewal of this covenant, binding God's people to Him through Christ's sacrifice.

Conclusion

From Genesis to Revelation, the Eucharist is foreshadowed, instituted, and celebrated as the supreme gift of God. The Old Testament prepares for it through Melchizedek, the Passover, and the manna. Jesus Himself promises it in John 6, institutes it at the Last Supper, and reveals His presence in the breaking of the bread at Emmaus. The apostles hand it on to the Church, making it central to Christian life.

The biblical foundations make clear that the Eucharist is not symbolic memory but a real participation in Christ's sacrifice and His abiding presence. It is the fulfillment of God's plan of salvation, the true Bread from heaven, and the covenant sealed in Christ's Blood. For this reason, the Church calls the Eucharist the "source and summit of the Christian life," the sacrament that contains the entire mystery of our faith.

Teachings from the Catechism of the Catholic Church

The **Catechism of the Catholic Church (CCC)** provides a comprehensive summary of the Church's faith regarding the Eucharist. Drawing on Scripture, the Fathers, Councils, and centuries of tradition, it presents the Eucharist as the "source and summit of the Christian life" (CCC 1324). What follows is a synthesis of its key teachings.

The Centrality of the Eucharist

The Catechism states that the Eucharist is the "sum and summary of our faith" (CCC 1327). All other sacraments are ordered toward it, and the Church's entire life flows from it. The Eucharist is celebrated as a memorial of Christ's death and Resurrection, a sacrifice, a meal, and a foretaste of the heavenly banquet. It is at once an act of thanksgiving, praise, and communion with Christ and His Church.

Names of the Sacrament

The Catechism lists several traditional names, each revealing a dimension of its mystery (CCC 1328–1332):

- **Eucharist** ("thanksgiving"), highlighting gratitude to God.

- **The Lord's Supper**, recalling the Last Supper and anticipating the heavenly banquet.

- **The Breaking of Bread**, a term used in the Acts of the Apostles.

- **The Eucharistic Assembly**, since it is celebrated by the gathered community.

- **The Holy Sacrifice**, because it makes present Christ's sacrifice on the Cross.

- **Holy Communion**, uniting us with Christ and with one another.

- **Holy Mass**, from *missa* — the sending forth of the faithful into the world.

Real Presence of Christ

One of the most important teachings of the Catechism is the doctrine of the **Real Presence**. Christ is truly, really, and substantially present in the Eucharist — Body, Blood, Soul, and Divinity (CCC 1374). This presence is not symbolic but actual, effected by the power of the Holy Spirit and the words of Christ spoken by the priest.

The Church uses the term **transubstantiation** to explain this change (CCC 1376). While the appearances of bread and wine remain, their substance is changed into the Body and Blood of Christ. This mystery is central to Catholic faith and devotion.

The Eucharist as Sacrifice

The Catechism emphasizes that the Eucharist is not only a meal but also a sacrifice (CCC 1365–1367). It makes present the one sacrifice of Christ on Calvary in an unbloody manner. The Mass is not a repetition of the Cross but its sacramental representation. The same Christ who offered Himself once for all is present and offered anew in every Mass.

In this way, the Eucharist is also the **sacrifice of the Church**. The faithful unite their lives, prayers, and sufferings with Christ's offering. As the bread and wine are presented at the altar, the people symbolically offer themselves to God, who transforms their sacrifice by uniting it with that of Christ.

The Eucharist as Communion

The Eucharist is also described as a **sacrament of unity** (CCC 1325, 1396). By receiving the Body of Christ, the faithful are united more closely with Him and with each other. Holy Communion forgives venial sins, strengthens charity, and preserves from future sin (CCC 1391–1395). It binds the faithful into one Body, the Church.

This unity requires proper disposition. The Catechism stresses that one must be in a **state of grace** to receive Communion worthily (CCC 1385). Grave sin requires sacramental confession before approaching the altar. In addition, the faithful observe the Eucharistic fast of one hour before Communion (CCC 1387).

The Eucharist and the Other Sacraments

The Eucharist is intimately linked to the sacraments of Christian initiation. Baptism incorporates a person into Christ, Confirmation strengthens the bond, and the Eucharist nourishes that life with Christ Himself (CCC 1322). The Eucharist also strengthens those receiving the sacraments of Holy Orders and Matrimony, giving grace for their vocations. For the sick and dying, **Viaticum** (the Eucharist received before death) serves as spiritual food for the final journey (CCC 1524–1525).

The Eucharist as Pledge of Glory

Finally, the Catechism presents the Eucharist as a foretaste of heaven (CCC 1402–1405). In receiving Christ's Body and Blood, the faithful anticipate the eternal banquet of the Kingdom of God. The Eucharist unites the Church on earth with the Church in heaven, joining the faithful to Mary, the saints, and all who have gone before. It nourishes hope and keeps alive the longing for eternal life with God.

Conclusion

The Catechism's teaching on the Eucharist shows it as sacrifice, presence, communion, and pledge of glory. It is thanksgiving, memorial, and the real Body and Blood of Christ. It is the center of Catholic life, drawing the faithful into deeper union with God and with one another.

By meditating on these truths, Catholics learn why the Eucharist is rightly called the "source and summit of the Christian life" (CCC 1324). Every Mass, every act of reverence toward the Blessed Sacrament, and every Holy Communion is a profound encounter with the living Christ who gives Himself for the salvation of the world.

Chapter 13 – Living the Mass Daily

The Eucharist is not simply an event we attend once a week on Sunday. It is the source and summit of the Christian life, meant to shape how we live every day. The graces received at Mass — union with Christ, forgiveness of venial sins, strength for the journey, and communion with the Church — are not confined to the liturgy. They are given so that we may carry Christ into our homes, workplaces, schools, and communities. Living the Mass daily means letting its prayers, gestures, and spirit guide our choices and actions, transforming ordinary life into a continuation of worship.

This way of life begins with small, intentional practices: reading and reflecting on the Scriptures proclaimed at daily Mass, cultivating devotion to the Eucharist through prayer, and making every action an offering to God. It extends to living in charity, seeking reconciliation, and bearing witness to the Gospel with integrity. By making space for the spirit of the liturgy each day, Catholics learn to see the presence of Christ not only on the altar but in every person they meet. In this way, the Mass is never finished; it continues in the life of the believer and the mission of the Church.

Daily Readings and Reflection

The Church provides a cycle of daily Scripture readings that form the foundation of prayer and reflection outside of Sunday Mass. These readings, found in the **Lectionary**, are arranged in a two-year cycle for weekdays and a three-year cycle for Sundays. They allow the faithful to journey through a broad portion of the Bible, hearing the Old Testament, the Psalms, the Gospels, and the letters of the New Testament in a rhythm that connects daily life with the mystery of salvation.

Reflecting on the daily readings helps Catholics bring the voice of God into their ordinary routines. Even if one cannot attend daily Mass, taking ten minutes to read the assigned passages and meditate on them keeps the heart aligned with the Church's prayer. Many Catholics use a missalette, a daily devotional, or online resources to follow the readings.

The practice of **lectio divina** (sacred reading) can deepen this reflection. This involves reading the Scripture slowly, meditating on a word or phrase that stands out, praying in response, and finally resting in God's presence. Over time, this habit forms a living dialogue with God, where His Word becomes a light for daily decisions.

By uniting daily prayer with the Church's liturgical readings, Catholics extend the grace of the Mass into their personal lives. Scripture becomes not only something proclaimed on Sunday but food for the soul every day of the week.

Eucharistic Adoration

Eucharistic Adoration is a devotion that flows directly from belief in the Real Presence of Christ in the Eucharist. If Jesus is truly present in the consecrated Host — Body, Blood, Soul, and Divinity — then it is fitting that the faithful spend time in prayer before Him outside of Mass. Adoration is an extension of the worship offered during the liturgy, giving believers a chance to remain in the presence of Christ, to gaze upon Him, and to rest in His love.

Adoration can take many forms. It may be simple, with the Blessed Sacrament reserved in the tabernacle, before which the faithful pray quietly. It can also be solemn, when the consecrated Host is placed in a monstrance and exposed on the altar. Some parishes hold regular hours of exposition, while others have perpetual adoration, ensuring that someone is always present in prayer before Christ.

During adoration, people pray in different ways: some recite the Rosary, others read Scripture, some use devotional books, and many simply sit in silence, offering their hearts to God. Adoration deepens personal love for Christ, strengthens faith, and fosters greater reverence for the Eucharist received at Mass. It is a school of prayer where the faithful learn to be still before God and let His presence transform them.

Bringing the Mass into Your Everyday Life

The celebration of the Eucharist is not meant to remain within the church walls. The graces received at Mass are intended to shape the daily lives of the faithful. Every word, gesture, and prayer in the liturgy is a call to live the Gospel in concrete ways.

Bringing the Mass into daily life begins with **thanksgiving**. Just as the Eucharist itself means "thanksgiving," Catholics are called to live with grateful hearts. Offering a morning prayer of thanks, saying grace before meals, and pausing at night to reflect on blessings are simple but powerful ways to extend the spirit of the Mass.

The Mass also teaches **sacrifice**. As bread and wine symbolize the offering of human labor, so Catholics are called to offer their work, joys, and sufferings to God each day. Acts of charity, patience, and service become extensions of the Eucharistic offering.

Living the Mass daily also involves **communion with others**. The faithful who receive Christ's Body are called to be His Body in the world, practicing forgiveness, reconciliation, and unity in families, workplaces, and communities.

Finally, the Mass inspires **mission**. The dismissal sends the faithful forth to announce the Gospel and glorify God by their lives. This mission is fulfilled not only by words but by example — living with integrity, kindness, and faith.

In these ways, the Eucharist is not only celebrated on Sundays but lived throughout the week, transforming ordinary life into a continual act of worship.

Made in the USA
Middletown, DE
15 October 2025